LOVESHOCK

How to Recover from a Broken Heart and Love Again

Stephen Gullo, Ph.D., and Connie Church

SIMON AND SCHUSTER
New York London Toronto
Sydney Tokyo

Loveshock is not intended as a psychotherapy, or in lieu of psychotherapy, for those seeking professional help. While it is a self-help guide and a system of personal coaching for those suffering from a love loss, we urge you to seek additional help from a mental health counselor if you feel that you are unable to cope with your loss.

Simon and Schuster
Simon & Schuster Building
Rockefeller Center
1230 Avenue of the Americas
New York, New York 10020

Published by the Simon & Schuster Trade Division
SIMON AND SCHUSTER and colophon are registered
trademarks of Simon & Schuster Inc.
Designed by Helen L. Granger/Levavi & Levavi
Manufactured in the United States of America

10 9 8 7 6 5 4 3 2 1

Library of Congress Cataloging in Publication Data

Gullo, Stephen
    Loveshock : how to survive a broken heart and love again.
    1. Separation (Psychology).   2. Love.   I. Church,
Connie   II. Title.
BF575.G7G85   1988   158'.2   88-11568
ISBN 0-671-64958-2

To the Love family: Lee, Matthew, Wendy, and Florence L., whose lives and deeds exemplify the name that they bear.

To Dr. Austin Kutscher, professor, scientist, and healer, whose work has influenced generations of health professionals in their effort to comfort those who suffer from loss.

—STEPHEN GULLO

To Al Lowman, my dear friend and agent, who truly lived every moment of this book's creation. Without your devotion, dedication and constant encouragement, Al, Loveshock *would not have been completed. Thank you from the bottom of my heart. And thank you for always being there for me.*

—CONNIE CHURCH

Contents

And the Lord is close to the brokenhearted . . .

ISAIAH

Preface

Oh, the tragic moments in history when love has gone wrong . . . Imagine Cleopatra with the asp clutched to her breast, Romeo and his Juliet dying so that they could in a sense live again, Henry VIII and his many unfortunate wives. And let us not forget how Van Gogh sliced off his ear and sent it to his true love. Songs have been written, great masterpieces painted, operas composed, ballets performed, novels written—all inspired by and depicting the agonies of a love loss. Artists have been moved to greatness as they tried to make sense of the many complexities of love—and especially, why love has to end. Is there anything more compelling, more painful in life than a broken heart?

I'll never forget the night I received a hysterical phone call from one of my dearest friends. It was eleven o'clock, and when I answered the phone Genevieve was barely audible as she sobbed, "Connie, this is Genevieve—it's awful! Can you come? I don't know what to do . . . I'm at the Beverly Hills Hotel, the Polo Lounge. Please hurry."

Before I could find out what had happened, she hung up the phone. As I drove to the hotel, all I could imagine was that someone very near and dear to her had died. What else could have possibly put her in such a state?

When I found her in the Polo Lounge I was shocked by what I saw. There sat one of Europe's favorite starlets, slumped over a large vodka, a pack of cigarettes, and a mass of papers, looking anything but glamorous.

Her silk jacket lay in a heap at her feet under the table; one strap of her dress was sliding off her shoulder. The beautiful blond curls were in a wild disarray and her big brown eyes, which had become her trademark, were full of such sadness and grief that I anticipated the worst. As I sat down beside her she crumpled in my lap.

"Genevieve, what's happened? Has somebody died— your mother? Is Claude all right?" I looked around, worried about the scene she was creating. Fortunately, when you're famous you can get away with almost anything.

Genevieve suddenly sat up again and reached for her vodka. After a healthy gulp she said, "It's love. Love has died and my heart is breaking. Ryan is ending our marriage."

I couldn't believe it. "But I thought you two had such a great, exotic life. The travel, the glamour—you're both so successful. And you have your wonderful son."

As she made an effort to gather the papers, she told me, "He says he no longer feels the electricity, the excitement. And can you believe that he actually served me with all these papers two weeks ago, before he even called me?" She bit her lip, trying to fight back the tears. She began to laugh uncontrollably, and then she cried as she looked at me through her haze of pain and said, "Oh, Connie, what am I going to do?"

I didn't know what to say. For me, the solution to any emotional crisis was to throw myself into my work. And so I asked her my obvious "What about your work?"

As the waiter placed another vodka before her, she gulped it down before the ice had a chance to melt and then uttered, "They want me in Rome . . . Italian miniseries. And believe it or not, I'm to play one of the most sought-after women in the world—the woman that everybody wants but nobody can have . . ."

By the time I left Genevieve, tucked in, with her baubles and jewels on the nightstand beside her bed, it was 6:00 A.M. The vodka had done the job—she was out cold, her emotional pain on hold. As I closed the door to her suite, all I could think of was how typically Hollywood this drama was—and before she knows it, I thought, there'll be another husband or boyfriend, this one forgotten in time. Something straight out of the tabloids.

As I drove home to my husband and two children, little did I know that I myself was about to suffer the anguish and emotional pain that comes with a broken heart. What I thought was just typical Hollywood drama had hit home. I too was about to experience the profound emptiness and sense of loss that fills one up when love changes course and splits the heart in half.

Four months after my evening with Genevieve, my husband, Jim, and I had separated and I was on my way back to New York City with my two children in tow. While I kept myself together and plastered a smile on my face for the sake of my children, my insides were churning and I felt like I was dying. I could barely eat or sleep and was filled with anxiety. During that long plane ride I flashed back to my night with Genevieve, and for the first time I truly connected with her pain. Now I understood. No wonder she had drunk herself into a stupor. Had it not been for my children, I might have done the same. Like Genevieve, I was suffering from a broken heart. The symptoms were so intense that it was hard for me to believe that the pain would ever end.

Fortunately, when I arrived in Manhattan, a concerned friend referred me to a wonderful psychotherapist, Dr. Stephen Gullo, who has developed a special therapy for mending broken hearts. Dr. Gullo took me under his wing and guided me through a course of therapy for what he calls *loveshock*—what each of us experiences in varying degrees when we have loved intensely and lost that love. Since his therapy is really a program of personal coaching, not a psychological therapy, Dr. Gullo had me consult a psychiatric colleague before we began. This was to make sure that there were no significant pathologies involved.

During the process of my own therapy I realized that the insights and survival skills Dr. Gullo had to offer to those of us struck by loveshock should be shared. So we decided to develop his remarkable loveshock therapy into a book—and who better to write it than someone who was experiencing the phenomenon herself?

People need to know that they are not alone in their suffering when a love relationship ends. In fact, it is a rare human being who, during the course of a lifetime, will not experience some degree of loveshock at least once, whether it is through death, divorce, or the breakup of a love relationship. The only uncertainty is at what point or under what conditions it will occur in your life.

What Dr. Gullo and I offer are guidelines to help you get through your loveshock crisis, as we explain to you why you feel the way you do (no, you are not going crazy!), what you can expect to feel as you go through each stage, how to get through it, and ultimately, how to get beyond it so that you can rebuild your life and love again. As you read this book, think of Dr. Gullo as your personal coach, easing you through your pain so that you can resume a happy, productive life. This is what Dr. Gullo's loveshock therapy did for me and what I believe this book can do for you.

CONNIE CHURCH

LOVESHOCK

Introduction

When choosing a topic for my doctoral dissertation as a Ph.D. candidate in psychology at Columbia University, I was drawn to the meaning of love and loss, especially the emotional conflict they create for all of us when love leads to loss. This was the beginning of a personal journey that led to the discovery and definition of the loveshock phenomenon—a phenomenon that I have documented and researched for over a decade.

In collaboration with my distinguished colleague, psychiatrist Dr. Ivan Goldberg, I started my research by observing the lives of sixteen very special women who were unwilling psychological travelers on the road from life to death. Their husbands were terminally ill. I entered each woman's life when she was told that her husband had a terminal diagnosis and I stayed with her until he actually died. The emotional pain that I observed in these women was overwhelming, as they permitted me to accompany them on this journey to death.

In studying their trauma of a profound love loss, I found in this most tragic human condition a window back to life, the perfect setting in which to understand how people let go of love relationships. I realized that what I learned in working with the bereaved could be practically applied to those who had been unlucky or unwise in love, that there were coping skills that they could develop to rebuild their emotional lives and ultimately find the courage and ability to love again.

My loveshock work actually began when one of the women from the group of sixteen called me about her daughter who was going through the trauma of breaking off with her lover. When she asked for my help I hesitated, telling her, "Well, I haven't had any experience practicing that type of therapy."

She quickly snapped back at me, "But you've had plenty of experience, Dr. Gullo. You've been studying all of us letting go of our love relationships as our husbands have died. This is just another form of letting go of a love relationship." Her insight helped me realize that what I had learned in working with the dying could help the living. Freud once observed that a good doctor learns from his patients, and she taught me; her comment gave me the confidence to take that step. I was successful with her daughter, my first loveshock patient.

I came up with the term *loveshock* because of the research I had done on Viet Nam soldiers who were suffering from shell shock. As I read about their psychological disorientation, their numbness, their fear of love, and their inability to enter intimate love relationships, I realized that in that intense moment of facing death they had prepared themselves to let go not only of their lives but of all their love relationships as well.

I recognized some notable parallels between the symptoms of soldiers going through shell shock and the symptoms of people letting go of love relationships. Like soldiers being shelled, the first thing that happened to people when a serious love relationship ended was that they went into a form of shock. And in this state of shock, they were in many ways similar to soldiers in shell shock: they were unable to sleep, unable to concentrate, unable to feel deep emotion for others. The more I thought about shell shock and the letting go of love, the clearer the connection became between love loss and shock. I also realized that the soldier suffering shell shock experienced, simultaneously, loveshock as well. For during those brief moments, confronting the possibility of imminent death, he would have to let go of everyone and everything that he loved.

However, it wasn't until I presented my loveshock theory at an international symposium on "Women and Loss" sponsored by the Foundation of Thanatology at the Columbia Presbyterian Medical Center in New York City in 1978 that I realized how universal this phenomenon is. National news tabloids and magazines took notice. I began to be invited on television talk shows and radio shows to discuss loveshock. My phone was ringing off the hook from people who declared that they were suffering from loveshock. They wanted to know how to get through it, to know if there was a cure.

As I began to observe my loveshock patients closely, I recognized recurring symptoms and stages that are determined by the degree of loveshock one experiences. While I had no cure to offer my patients, I could help them make sense of what they were experiencing—make them realize that they could endure what they initially found to be unbearable.

There were guidelines they could follow that would help them to influence their personal outcome in a way that would lessen their emotional pain. I could teach them emotional survival skills, by helping them to understand the predictable course their loveshock would take and the possible stumbling blocks they might encounter along the way. When practiced, these emotional survival skills could get them through the most difficult periods of their loveshock, as they allowed their love-wounds to heal. However, I didn't want to downplay the motivation it would take on their part to get them through this time of emotional chaos.

Finally, I found that I could provide them with the necessary tools for rebuilding their lives as they prepared not just to love again, but to love well. With my personal coaching, as well as the skills and tools I had to offer, my patients could in a sense create their own cure depending on their personal needs.

Although I refer to the people I have treated for loveshock as my patients, it would be more accurate to describe them as students learning life skills that are vital to their emotional growth and development. Truly, loveshock therapy is a system of personal coaching, *not* a psychotherapy. I make this point because while you may feel as if you are going insane at different times during loveshock, it is not a form of mental illness: loveshock is an inevitable *process* for very nearly all of us.

As you read this book and take yourself through your loveshock experience, know that what I offer comes from years of research and intense sharing with my "students." There is no instant remedy, nor should there be! Love is one of the most profound human experiences, and severing a lovebond is one of life's most painful tasks. We cannot anesthetize ourselves to the pain of life without also anesthetizing ourselves to the joy of life— much of which encompasses loving. To feel deep emotional pain because of a love loss is an indication of your great capacity to love.

When you become deeply involved in a love relationship, you expose a part of yourself that very few people will ever know. This is what psychoanalyst Dr. Rollo May calls "the courage of love." And this is why you feel so much pain when a love relationship ends.

Yes, it takes courage to love. As you, open and vulnerable, share your innermost feelings and emotions with another person, there is an element of risk involved. And ultimately, whether through death or through breakup, loveshock is almost unavoidable.

While each stage of the loveshock experience can contain many painful moments for you, you can emerge stronger and wiser for all that you have endured. For in life, not only is there destructive pain but there is growth pain as well, which enables us to become stronger and more competent human beings. Loveshock is part of the growth pain of life, and by learning to manage and master it you will develop a coping skill that is central to living: the capacity to accept a loss and recover from it, realizing that you are still whole as you continue to live a full life, and I hope, love again.

CHAPTER ONE

Understanding Loveshock

The Queen sobbed hysterically, pacing the palace floors. As she wailed into the silence of the night, the chambermaids looked at one another in fear. Special doctors had been called to her side, but nothing could be done to ease her grief. Mediums had been summoned, but it was impossible to raise Prince Albert from the dead. He was gone and she was powerless over his death—a fact she found unbearable.

As the weeks passed, the palace slowly became Queen Victoria's prison. For within those walls there was no escape from the memory of Albert or the realization that she would never hold his hands again, hear his voice, or know the pleasure of his embrace. Finally, overwhelmed by her memories and her inconsolable grief, she fled Buckingham Palace and ruled for the next thirty years from her self-imposed exile. She became known as the Widow of Windsor, clad in widow's weeds, drifting among the royal homes of Windsor, Osborne, and Balmoral.

So great was her loss that she put the entire British Empire into loveshock. The somber clothing, the austerity, the rigidity—the Victorian age was in truth an age of mourning, a reflection of Queen Victoria's grief, of her own loveshock.

Throughout their marriage, Jennifer lived with her husband's infidelities, his unfulfilled promises, and the hope that he would change. Rick was a promising young film director when they met, and she had stuck with him through thick and thin as he made his way to the top. Two children and twenty years later, as she sat in the library of her Malibu mansion, she realized that this was the last time she would ever wait for him to come home. She knew that there was another woman in his life—the call girl who was always on hand for the production company that he owned—but she wanted to believe that she came first. As the minutes passed painfully into hours, the grandfather clock loudly declared each one that passed.

When the phone finally rang, she picked it up breathlessly. She was sure that it was Rick. Instead it was the gardener, inquiring whether she wanted to plant perennials or annuals in the south bed. Jennifer barely got through the conversation when she dropped to the floor in a sobbing heap. It was at that moment that she realized she was married to a hope, not a reality, and went into loveshock.

The following morning, as her housekeeper packed her bags and helped her move into the Bel-Air Hotel, Jennifer was in a state of shock. Fortunately, her children were away at boarding school. Numb with emotional pain, she placed the Do Not Disturb sign on the door and withdrew into seclusion. Phone calls went unanswered, and she could not remember what happened from one day to the next. She kept the shades drawn, so that she never knew if it was day or night. As grief overwhelmed Jennifer, everything in her life seemed fuzzy and vague. For weeks she could barely eat or sleep.

Although Jennifer chose to leave Rick, she felt as if she had lost a part of herself. But to stay would have meant losing everything, because as each day passed she felt that she was being emotionally unraveled and diminished as a human being.

Immersed in her shock and grief, she knew that she had to bury her dream. And still, when she spoke of her love for Rick, she would say passionately, "If I had only one breath of life left, I would give it to him." It took Jennifer two years to recover from her loveshock experience.

It was Valentine's Day in New York. Standing by the open window, David gazed blankly down at the busy streets. The cold air stung his tear-streaked face. He wasn't sure if he had the nerve to jump, and yet the thought of living without Vanessa was more than he could bear. A promising young lawyer, who had proudly worked two jobs to pay his way through law school, David had everything to live for—except love.

Having never experienced open affection or love from his parents, as they were too busy struggling to clothe and feed their five children, David was sure that he had finally found emotional fulfillment in his relationship with Vanessa. This certainly had made it all the more painful when she had called him out of the blue four weeks earlier and broken off their engagement. Since that time he had felt totally abandoned and had not been able to function. Even the simplest of tasks seemed difficult to complete. Often he sat dazed and crying, forgetting what he had done the moment before. Unable to concentrate on his work, David had lost a routine case, which escalated his sense of worthlessness.

He had tried to block his pain with liquor, had flirted with cocaine, and had engaged in several one-night stands, hoping to remove Vanessa from his heart forever. But all he had achieved were bad hangovers, a lot of empty sex, and more loneliness. It seemed that the harder he tried to forget about her, the more she invaded his thoughts.

As his emotional pain gnawed at his insides, David listlessly walked across the room and flipped on his television. Slowly turning from one station to the next, he finally settled on a midday talk show. He hoped that the voices would give him some comfort and if not, that he would at least be able to gather enough courage to jump. Deeply in loveshock, David was sure that he was the only person in the world who felt the way that he did. He was convinced that he was alone in the intensity of his pain, that his broken heart separated him from the rest of the world. His loveshock had pushed him to the edge.

THE LOVESHOCK PHENOMENON

As dramatic as these stories sound, they are all true. Queen Victoria's case is an extreme example of the most obvious kind of loveshock—suffering a love loss through death. However, in our day and age, when divorce is almost as common as marriage and people have the opportunity for several love relationships in the course of their lives, loveshock occurs most frequently through the breakup of a relationship.

Those of you who are experiencing or have experienced loveshock can probably relate to some or several parts of these stories—especially Jennifer's and David's. I want to emphasize that as devastating as it can be to go through, *loveshock is a normal phenomenon with a predictable course of symptoms, stages, and events, for which there is typically a beginning and an end.*

Specifically, loveshock is that state of psychological numbness, disorientation, and emptiness that you experience following the breakup of a serious love relationship. No two individuals experience loveshock in exactly the same way, however, because human behavior varies so much from one individual to another. Usually the first loveshock crisis you experience is the most severe because you haven't developed the coping skills to manage it. I have also found that the degree of loveshock you experience is directly proportional to the intensity of your involvement in a love relationship. You can experience many breakups in the course of a lifetime, but if you are not deeply involved you will not go through an intense loveshock experience: you may feel some sadness, but you will not experience the degree of emotional pain that is characteristic of deep loveshock.

While I have found that it takes most people about one year to complete their loveshock experience, it is not unusual for recovery to take longer. Usually the time required, what I refer to as your *traveling time,* is determined by the amount of time you have spent with the other person and the depth of your commitment. For instance, couples who have been living together or seeing each other for just a year will have a shorter loveshock experience than couples who have been together for a few years. And couples divorcing after twenty or more years, with children, are likely to have the longest loveshock experience of all.

Whether or not it is normal for you to spend one, two, even three years in loveshock depends on how well you are functioning. If you are able to maintain your emotional center, act and react to situations reasonably, and motivate yourself through your daily routines, it is still not abnormal for your sadness and emotional pain to go on for a couple of years. What's important is that you continue to function—following the initial shock—while your lovewounds heal.

Many of my loveshock patients come to me at the onset of their loveshock because they are unable to function and feel as if they are emotionally unraveling. They are unable to concentrate and unable to sleep, and they have a sense of hopelessness. This initial inability to function is a normal result of their shock and grief. In fact, they are surprised when I tell them that their emotional state is appropriate, that the reason they are in so much pain is that they are in touch with their loss—and that this is healthy! But, I tell them, they must begin to confront their pain and move themselves through it. For them to bear the "unbearable," to face the loveshock experience head-on, by working their way through it and by understanding it—this forcing themselves to function is the beginning of their healing process.

Loveshock does not become pathological unless you try to repress it or inhibit it through denial or different forms of excess, such as drug and alcohol abuse. Failure to recognize and express your emotional pain can severely impair your psychological health and your ability to form new love relationships in the future. You may fear that the very same sequence of events will be repeated in your next relationship, or worse, you may doubt your ability to love. However, confronting your loveshock experience and learning from what went wrong in the relationship can turn the pain into a growth experience and provide you with insights and coping skills that can enhance your next relationship.

The repercussions of unresolved loveshock can damage more than your emotional health. When your life is filled with emotional pain and you don't deal with the accompanying feelings, the signal is put out to your body that you don't want to recover. Recent medical studies show that the stress created by unresolved grief, depression, and despair can depress the body's immune system, making you more susceptible to illness.

So loveshock, although painful, is a sign of health, and the *only* way to recover from loss of love. Not to feel loveshock after suffering from a significant love loss is to be disconnected from your emotions; to feel it is to be in touch with a very painful reality—but one that is vital to your emotional well-being.

WHAT TO EXPECT DURING A LOVESHOCK CRISIS

Jennifer and David both sought psychiatric help but were struggling to get beyond their loveshock until they came to me for therapy. In fact, what helped to prevent David from taking that fatal jump on Valentine's Day was that, by coincidence, I was on the talk show that he was watching, discussing the symptoms and stages of loveshock. He later told me that as he sat and listened to my description of loveshock, what he heard was exactly what he was experiencing at that moment and had been experiencing ever since the awful call from Vanessa. For the first time he was able to make sense of his experience and took comfort in knowing that there was a label for what he felt. He was dumbfounded to discover that what he was feeling was not unique, that millions of others had already suffered from the same symptoms and that many of them had gone on to love again. That day, learning what would happen next and that the pain he was feeling would not last forever kept him from jumping.

When I tell my patients, "This is what you are going through, and this is what you can expect next," it is as though a tremendous burden has been lifted from them. As they begin to understand the dynamics of their loveshock experience, their knowledge gives them an insight that helps them manage their fears as they constructively work their way through the experience. They also take a great deal of comfort in knowing that they are not alone, that I have treated many other people for loveshock, and yes, that these other people have lived through the experience. And perhaps most reassuring of all for them is to learn that the intensity of pain they are feeling at the moment will eventually decrease and even come to an end, that there will be a predictable course of events, a series of stages that they will go through that will enable them to reach that end.

Symptomatically, there are a wide range of symptoms that can be experienced at any given time by people suffering from loveshock. You may find yourself bingeing on food or alcohol and popping pills or taking drugs. As you react compulsively, what you are really seeking is a medicine to dull your pain, a balm to soothe your lovewounds. Unfortunately, there is no magic cure!

There can be waves of nausea and a loss of appetite.

You may become depressed and experience uncontrollable crying jags. Although extremely fatigued, you may
be unable to sleep. You may find that it is difficult for
you to concentrate, that you suffer from memory loss;
you may feel as if you have little or no energy. If you
drive, exercise great caution, as you may drive less at-
tentively and at times even recklessly.

When you are suffering from loveshock you often
wander through your daily routine unable to remember
what you have done. The only thing you seem able to
focus on is the other person and the relationship that
once was. In your obsessional thinking, every aspect of
your life can be invaded by thoughts of the other person.
As your thoughts become locked on the other person
and your pain, you just can't seem to break through and
get beyond them. You'll try anything to get that other
person out of your thoughts.

You may become totally reclusive, like Jennifer, re-
treating into seclusion and terrified of any involvement
with the opposite sex. Or conversely, like David, you
may plunge into an orgy of promiscuity. When you're
in loveshock, your life can become uncontrollable.

The most acute symptom you can expect to experience, the one that all the other symptoms feed off, is
that inner emptiness deep inside of you. You feel as if
you've lost a part of yourself, that something has been
wrenched from you. All of your feelings are intensified
as you are embraced by the loneliness of your life without the other person. And you are overcome by your
fear, fear that you will spend the rest of your life void
of any tenderness and affection, cut off from love—the
love that you want to give, the love that you need to
have.

TRAVELING THROUGH THE SIX STAGES OF LOVESHOCK

The symptoms of loveshock progress in a predictable pattern that can be broken down into six stages: *shock, grief, setting blame, resignation* (the "goodbye" stage), *rebuilding,* and *resolution.*

The rate at which you move from one stage to the next is what I call your *psychological traveling time.* Some of you will travel through these stages quickly, while others of you will travel through them slowly. Regardless of your traveling time, as you travel through each stage the intensity of the symptoms will begin to lessen. During shock, grief, and setting blame you suffer the most; by the time you have reached the final stage of resolution, your pain has faded into the past like a bad dream. But you *must* go through all the stages to resolution. One of the goals of loveshock therapy is to help you effectively manage your emotional pain so that you don't lock in to any of the stages that precede resolution.

It is also important to keep in mind that although there are common patterns, human behavior is not linear. There are many different ways that you can travel through the stages. For instance, as you move from one stage to the next, it is not unusual for vestiges of the previous stage to remain with you. Or you may spend a considerable amount of time traveling back and forth between two stages—what I call *the zigzag effect.* You may experience certain stages more intensely than others, or you may have a relatively brief experience with one stage and a prolonged experience with another. While it is important that you complete each stage and travel on to the next, allow yourself to flow with the process.

Don't be surprised if you zigzag several times throughout your loveshock experience.

There are no "right" or "wrong" ways to travel through the stages, but you should be alert to any self-destructive behaviors and attitudes that may develop because of the pain, regret, or guilt that you feel associated with your loss. I call these the *love pitfalls*. They include various compulsive behaviors such as food bingeing, excessive drinking, and promiscuity. I will discuss them in further detail in Chapter Five. These love pitfalls are setbacks that can occur along the way and will only delay, not prevent, your arrival at the final stage of resolution. There's nothing to feel guilty about if you have setbacks, nor does it matter how often they occur. What's important is that you recover as quickly as possible, get back on your feet, and continue to move forward. As you push yourself foward and as time passes, the setbacks will occur less frequently. Always keep in mind that you are going to come through this experience and that setbacks are normal.

The following description of the six stages of loveshock will give you a good idea of what you *may* experience with each stage.

Shock

At the onset of loveshock you feel an immediate sense of numbness, disorientation, and disbelief. Your life seems to stand still as you focus on your loss. You may be unable to eat, unable to sleep; it's as though you have become a zombie. The intensity of your feelings and the sense of acute loss block out all other concerns and activities. Later, when you look back on this period of your loveshock experience, you may have little recollection of what went on. Jennifer doesn't remember her housekeeper packing her bags or the drive to the Bel-Air Hotel. The weeks she spent locked away in the hotel are a distant blur in her memory. A protective stage, shock actually insulates you from the full impact of the emotional trauma you are experiencing.

Your shock can last for a day or it can last for a month—but rarely longer. It is eventually pushed out of the way by the breaking through of your emotions: your overwhelming sense of loss and grief.

Grief

When grief sets in you are not just mourning for the loss of the person. You're also mourning for all the time you shared, for the dreams that you mutually held in your hearts, and for the unfulfilled promise of a life together. You may also mourn for your own failure, realizing that no matter how hard you try or wish it to be, you alone cannot make a love relationship: it takes two willing partners.

As you deal with your loss, and the pain it generates in your life, you may feel irritable and short-tempered, snapping at friends and coworkers. You usually find yourself unresponsive to offers from friends to "fix you up" with dates because you need to complete your grief first. You may even be angry that your friends don't understand your need to grieve. This is not the right time for you to try to involve yourself in a new relationship.

As you grieve, you may have the compulsion to telephone the other person just so that you can hear his or her voice. You are desperate to maintain some sort of connection, no matter how unrealistic it is. But after you hear the initial hello you hang up, unable to speak a word to the person with whom you could at one time speak forever. David confessed to me, with great embarrassment, that he used to call Vanessa at 1:00 A.M. because she was half asleep and would say hello several times before hanging up. But he also felt hurt that she could sleep while he was suffering and wide awake. Magnifying his own pain, he was convinced that because she was sleeping, she was adjusting well and going on with her life.

Depression often develops at this time, as you are overwhelmed with a sense of hopelessness. It is not unusual to become locked in this stage. When this happens you lose more than the person you have loved— you lose yourself. If Queen Victoria hadn't spent thirty years locked in her grief, she probably could have married again. While she might never have been able to find another Prince Albert, she might have found someone else to share her life with.

When locked in grief, people often need and seek help. It is at this point that Jennifer began her loveshock therapy. We discovered, together, that one of the reasons she was unable to get beyond her grief was that she was afraid that no one would want her. After twenty years of marriage she felt used up: as painful as it was, grief was the "safest" place for her to be.

Setting Blame

When the hysteria of your grief subsides you have a psychological need to make sense of what has happened. It is at this time that you start analyzing what went wrong and you progress into the third stage of setting blame. You begin to confront the different problems as you struggle to understand what precipitated the breakup. You start to ask yourself, "What happened? Where did I go wrong? Where did he (or she) go wrong? Where did we go wrong?" You may blame yourself, the other person, or others in general for the breakup. You may look to your general life circumstances as well—stress on the job, an ill-timed move, financial problems, health problems—to place the blame.

Along with your hurt, the strongest emotion you will feel at this time is usually anger, and it may be acted out with various compulsive behaviors—bingeing, alcohol abuse, drug abuse, and promiscuity.

Your anger may be directed at the other person for the hurt that he or she has caused you, or at yourself, as you consider yourself a failure. David's sudden, atypical behavior of one-night stands, debauchery, and near suicide was his way of dealing with his anger. He blamed himself, so his anger was self-destructive. He was convinced that the breakup was his fault because he wasn't worthy of love. After all, although his parents had done their best, they had never shown him any real affection, so why would a beautiful woman life Vanessa want to marry him? Because he was placing all the blame on himself, David's self-esteem was at its lowest point when he consulted with me.

Out of anger, you may also enter into another relationship where subconsciously you take out on the other person the hurt and pain you feel within. You may be verbally abusive, physically aloof or just disrespectful of the other person's needs. I call this *revenge loving,* as you act out on the other person whatever you feel has been done to you.

It is not uncommon to travel back and forth between setting blame and grief before you are ready to move on to the fourth stage of resignation. Jennifer found herself doing this. One day she would be mourning all that she had lost, and then a few days later she would come to me in a rage, saying, "If only he had bothered to call all those times that he said he would! I could have continued, if there had been phone calls. How little I must have mattered to him that I didn't even merit a phone call!" I saw her anger as healthy and was able to use it as a means to take her out of her grief. As she expressed her anger, she realized that she deserved a lot more than she had gotten from her marriage. Using her anger constructively, she was slowly on her way to rebuilding her self-esteem.

Resignation—The Goodbye Stage

Traveling from setting blame to resignation may be the hardest transition of your loveshock experience. I like to call this stage *the goodbye stage* because it is the point at which you are able to say, "This person is no longer in my life. I can spend my life mourning or being angry, or I can push myself to go forward." Not only must you accept that the relationship is over, you must release it completely, detaching yourself from the other person and withdrawing the energy that you invested in the relationship. This is a bittersweet time during your loveshock experience, as you say goodbye to the relationship and all the feelings that have been involved in maintaining it. You may have mixed emotions—at once relieved that you are ready to let go and sad that you have to let go.

While it may sound as if the worst is over once you've reached resignation, it is not uncommon to get stuck in this stage. Perhaps you have little or no life motivation left because you are so drained. You may really have to push yourself to move on to rebuilding.

Although David was finally able to detach from Vanessa, in some ways he felt more fatigued and drained than he had during any other part of his loveshock experience. As he so aptly put it, "I feel as if a vampire, no, vampiress, has sucked all the blood out of me— discarding me to go on to the next victim!" Because of the emptiness he still felt, it was impossible for him to move on to rebuilding enthusiastically.

While the senior partners at David's law firm had already lessened his caseload, they eventually suggested that he take a vacation. Perhaps a trip would renew his usual vigor and the fighting spirit they all admired. David followed their advice, and although he couldn't afford anything lavish, found that just getting away from it all and going camping for a week was beneficial. When he returned he felt more energetic and was finally ready to make a fresh start, as he began to rebuild his life.

Rebuilding

Once you have begun to actively rebuild your life, the worst of your loveshock experience begins to recede. At this point you realize that you have more happy days than sad days. Your concentration is back and you're working on correcting any compulsive habits that you've developed during your loveshock experience. Your life is yours again and your focus is on re-creating its equilibrium. You're ready to date; you want to get out and really start to live. And some of you are focusing on your own needs for the first time in your life, selective about whom you'll spend your time with so that you can love in a healthy, balanced way.

At this point of her loveshock experience, Jennifer suddenly realized that she was laughing a lot, going out with her friends, and just enjoying her life. She was even open to the possibility of a new relationship. She had come a long way since her initial weeks of seclusion at the Bel-Air Hotel.

When she accepted a date for the first time in twenty years, she felt very strange. She never thought she'd be interested in dating again or, for that matter, that anyone would want to date her. But it got easier, and she actually started to enjoy her life as a single person. At first she found herself comparing every man she went out with to Rick, in personality as well as physically. I call this *comparison shopping*. I reminded her that while people may share certain similarities, each person is essentially unique. Whenever she started to compare, I had her shift her focus to what was different about the man she was dating and what needs she had that this person could or could not fulfill. We discussed things that they did that made their time together special. The more confident she became, the less comparing she did. When she met Tony, who became her second husband, she was able to know him in his own right, not in terms of how he related to Rick.

For many, rebuilding is like learning to walk again after having broken a leg. You've mended, but you need to build your strength by developing your self-esteem and confidence. Often your social and dating skills have to be polished. You can expect to make a few mistakes along the way.

While you are still aware of all the pain that you have been through, you begin to understand what you have gained and what you have lost because of the breakup. For many of you, what you have gained is greater than what you have lost. And for the rest, you will have the opportunity to create a happier, richer life as you continue to develop a greater awareness of yourself and your self-worth.

Resolution

This is the beginning of a new life cycle. You have resolved the conflict and the turmoil that have been with you since your loveshock experience first began. In a sense, you've made peace with your emotional pain. Your life is back on course again, but it's a different course because of the personal growth that occurred as you traveled through all of the stages of loveshock. At this time you may choose to begin a new love relationship. If not, you have more confidence in your ability to create your own happiness and take care of yourself.

For Jennifer, the resolution stage did include a new love relationship. When she came to me for what turned out to be her last session, she told me the following story. "Tony and I were having dinner in Malibu, and who should I see sitting across the room? None other than Rick and his call girl girlfriend—Laura!"

At this point in the story, Jennifer had a pensive look on her face. I was afraid she was going to tell me that she created a scene. She continued, "You're not going to believe what I did, Dr. Gullo. I actually got up, walked across the room, and said hello to my ex-husband and introduced myself to his girlfriend. Can you believe it? I politely stuck out my hand and said, 'Hi, I'm Jennifer Wexler. You must be Laura.' After some chitchat, I held my head high and walked back to my table. And do you know that I overheard Laura say, 'The lady is a real class act'? I could hardly believe my ears, but I felt a sense of pride and wholeness. And Tony was amazed by my courage to confront pleasantly two people who had caused me so much pain."

Jennifer was beaming as she finished telling me what happened and how happy Tony made her. I too was amazed that she could put her loveshock experience and all of its pain in the past and take such a courageous step. Now it was my turn to comment, "Your love-shock experience is over; there is no need for you to continue therapy."

PASSIVE-ACTIVE RESPONSE PATTERNS

One of the intial challenges you must overcome during the early stages of loveshock is to realize that while the relationship has ended, your life hasn't. At this time it is important that you evaluate your response pattern to your loveshock crisis. I have found that most people respond in extremes, either passively or actively. Your goal at this time should be to monitor your behavior so that you can manage your pain and maintain balance in your life.

When your response is passive, you withdraw into yourself and become reclusive. Your seclusion becomes your safety net as you keep yourself locked in the second stage of grief. A victim of your fear, you may be overwhelmed by dread of what the future will bring. Filled with self-doubt, your mind spins anxiously: "What will happen next? Who will ever want to love me again? Will I ever be loved again? How will I go on?" Queen Victoria's self-imposed exile for thirty years is an extreme example of a passive response pattern. Fleeing to the Bel-Air Hotel, Jennifer felt that grief was the safest place for her to be. She had been able to take the initial step to end her painful relationship with Rick, but she could go no further because she was paralyzed by her fear.

Conversely, when your response to your loveshock experience is active, you literally act out your pain on yourself and others. Instead of becoming reclusive and withdrawn, you are more likely to act compulsively and erratically. Food bingeing, alcohol abuse, drug abuse, and promiscuity are typical compulsive behaviors. So great is your pain, so low your sense of self-worth that you may take your active response pattern to the extreme and embark on a journey of self-destruction. Remember David—his heavy drinking and drug abuse combined with his numerous one-night stands—eventually standing by his window as he contemplated jumping?

While it's normal to spend some time both passively and actively responding in extremes to your loveshock experience, it is very important to evaluate the degree and frequency of these behaviors on a daily basis. An effective way to do this is what I call *self-monitoring.*

Self-monitoring can be done by recording your feelings on tape, keeping a journal, or making a list of the day's activities and how you felt while doing them. Or you can just take ten minutes twice a day to have an internal dialogue with yourself about what you are doing, how you feel, and how you think you are doing.

Think of self-monitoring as an opportunity to step outside of yourself and watch what's going on. The self-awareness and self-knowledge you gain from it can enhance your personal growth during loveshock. And if you are totally honest with yourself, self-monitoring will alert you to any destructive patterns or habits that are forming. This exercise is not intended to make you feel bad about yourself. It is intended to help you grow from your mistakes and move you through loveshock with a minimal amount of pain.

Since Jennifer, reacting passively, was stuck in the second stage of grief, I suggested that she keep a journal and actually monitor her grief. This proved to be very constructive and helped her move on to the next stage of setting blame. She found in her journal an effective catharsis as she purged her feelings, writing pages and pages about all the hurt and humiliation she felt she had endured, especially during the last five years of her marriage to Rick. Keeping a journal also helped her pinpoint her fears of what the future would bring, specifically, of never being loved again. Once she acknowledged her fears they became less frightening and she began to work on overcoming them. Jennifer was functioning again as she began to manage her loveshock.

This exercise and the other exercises and therapies I offer in this book should effectively move you through your loveshock experience and help you remain emotionally, mentally, and physically intact. However, if you spend more than a couple of weeks in extreme passive or active response patterns, you should seek additional help from your physician, therapist, or family counselor.

CHAPTER TWO

Confronting Your Fears

In working with people going through loveshock, I have developed a great awe for the power of the human psyche, its determination to survive and heal itself, especially when properly directed through self-help or with the guidance of a counselor or therapist. While your emotional pain may at times seem unbearable, there is a natural resilience within you to go on and work your way through it. It is this ability to endure emotional trauma that helps all of us to survive.

When you first go into loveshock, the numbness of shock protects you from the full impact of the emotional blow you've just received. It is as though your psyche has put itself on hold to prepare itself to deal with an overwhelming and often tragic reality. This pause allows your psyche to marshal its resources and defenses before actually confronting the emotional pain at hand— a kind of psychological retreat before the advance.

However, as your shock begins to subside and you move into the second stage of grief, your fears begin to emerge and may even overwhelm you. You start to deal with the reality of your situation: an important love relationship is no longer a part of your life. It is important that you accept your fears as a natural and normal dynamic of loveshock; know that everyone who experiences loveshock is going to have to confront certain fears. And any anxiety, panic, or despair connected with your fears is predictable. You are not alone and you are not going crazy!

While loveshock can trigger a wide variety of fears during any of its stages, including fears from your childhood that you thought you had resolved, there are some common ones that I see in many of my loveshock patients. You may find that you experience just one or two of these fears or all of them. Know that in your own loveshock, some or all of these fears will probably occur. In this way you can prepare yourself and find it easier to cope. This knowledge will not diminish the pain, but it will provide you with greater control because you will understand what's happening. Keeping your fears under control will help you manage your pain more effectively. Use your knowledge to conduct a mental "fire drill" in which you rehearse what to do, reflect on what's working and what's not working, and anticipate what might happen next.

THE GREATEST FEAR OF ALL

The first and greatest fear you confront occurs in the second stage of grief. You may well be terrified that you'll always feel the way you do at the moment—that the intense emotional pain you are experiencing will never go away and that the terrible empty pit of lone-

liness you feel will engulf you forever. You fear that
because of it, you will never be able to move forward
to really live and love again. As you are filled with self-
doubt, thoughts of "I'll never find someone else" or "I
don't have the ability to make a love relationship work"
eat away at you.

What you must do during these intense periods of fear
is to live moment to moment, easing yourself through
your daily routines, and trust that with time your emotional pain will become less intense. Fortunately, as a
protective mechanism, the human psyche naturally di-
minishes painful memories with the passage of time;
otherwise you would be unable to function. To constantly relive acute, vivid memories of every negative
experience would eventually drive you to real insanity,
as you would be in a perpetual state of fear. (I will discuss
this in greater detail in Chapter Four: Your Loveshock
Traveling Time.)

Most of my patients find these intense periods of fear
to be some of the most difficult moments of their loveshock experience, moments during which they feel that
they are losing their minds, that they are out of control,
that they just can't go on. In rare instances the temporary
insanity brought on by this fear can push a person over
the edge.

This was true for Earlene, a massage therapist orig-
inally from Barbados. She was so afraid that her emotional pain would never go away that she tried to take
her own life. Because she was not responding to traditional therapy, her internist, a colleague who once
worked with me at the medical center where I trained,
asked me to consult on her case. As I sat beside her
hospital bed, she began to tell me her story.

Her first marriage had been nothing more than a business arrangement so that she could get her green card to live and work in the United States. This marriage had ended by mutual agreement, and she had never experienced loveshock. Twenty-five years later at forty-five years old, Earlene met Ed. She knew that she had finally found the love of her life. A good-looking police sergeant, he became the center of her world.

She scheduled her days off to coincide with his and made herself available to fulfill his every need. Being a police sergeant, he was often on call, so their time together was infrequent and unpredictable. But the moments they did share were romantic and unforgettable.

"We'd have a little sherry and dance by candlelight to our favorite records before dinner. All Ed had to do was look into my eyes and I could just feel myself filling up with love. I've never felt this way about anyone or anything in my whole life. When we made love it was so incredible that I swear the earth stopped. He always made me feel so beautiful and special. It didn't bother him that I was middle-aged and a little overweight, because as he always said, 'Our souls connect.' While everything seemed perfect between us, the one thing I never understood was why we would never spend any time at his place. I guess deep down inside I suspected that he was married, but I couldn't understand how someone so perfect for me could belong to anyone else. So I just looked the other way. Finally, a little more than a year after we had first met, the truth came out. Not only was he married, but he had three sons."

"And you felt that you had to end it, even though having him in your life made you so happy?"

"Oh, Dr. Gullo, I just couldn't go on. Although I married so I could live in the United States, I was raised to believe that adultery is wrong no matter what the circumstances. And while I was married, even though I wasn't in love, I was never with another man. I guess I'm old-fashioned, but this is a value that sticks to me like glue. I can't go against it—but I'm miserable without him . . ."

"Then I would think that you would be proud of yourself for staying true to your values. It's a wonderful quality, Earlene—to have the courage of your convictions. Some people spend a lifetime trying to develop this quality and never even come close. You've also realized that shared values are necessary if you are to have a happy love relationship."

As she looked away, toward the white hospital wall, she said, "A lot of good the courage of my convictions does me. I can't bear the pain of not having him in my life anymore, and that's why I took all those pills. The emptiness was killing me, so I thought why not just finish the job instead of prolonging my grief."

"How do you feel now, Earlene?"

"Empty. Lost. I'm so afraid. I gave him a piece of my heart—and now it's gone."

While Earlene's story was as unique and as special as Earlene herself, I had heard her final analysis of her feelings many times before. Like so many other love-shock patients, locked in the second stage of grief, she was convinced that her pain would never end. What she needed now was something to hold on to, something that could help move her loveshock. Fortunately she had a career that meant a lot to her.

"Tell me about your work as a massage therapist."

"Oh, I just love helping people and making them feel good. You know, Dr. Gullo, massage therapy is a wonderful thing. It can help you relax when life gets tough. And it can even strengthen your immune system."

"Sounds like massage therapy might help you right now."

"Why yes, I guess I've been pretty tough on myself. And what I must have done to my body with all those pills! And you know, I've really neglected my clients over the last couple of months. Some of them are long-standing clients who have really counted on me for years. I've been a massage therapist for twenty-one years . . ."

Earlene still had a lot of grief and sadness to work through, but her pain became manageable as she poured all the extra energy she had expended on Ed back into her work. By helping others she was helping herself. The emptiness that had devastated her at the beginning of her loveshock slowly diminished. Six months later she called me to report, "You were right, Dr. Gullo, the pain has faded. I still miss Ed—I got rid of all of our favorite records—but things don't seem so bad anymore. I've also managed to take off ten pounds and feel pretty good about myself . . ."

LOSING YOUR EMOTIONAL CENTER

In the early stages of loveshock, the second stage of grief and the third stage of setting blame, emotional outbursts and even hysteria can be expected. Because you are so emotionally vulnerable at this time, you may even find yourself suddenly crying for no apparent reason. Or it may happen that a song on the radio, a favorite television show that you once shared, and even certain times of the day can trigger these outbursts. The intensity of these outbursts may really frighten you: your emotional reactions are running to extremes.

Many of my loveshock patients start therapy with me

at this time because they feel that they are losing the very center of their being. They are afraid that they will emotionally unravel into nothingness because they are unable to maintain their self-control.

During the first month of her loveshock, Marjorie remembers bursting into tears when a cab driver simply asked her, "Where to, lady?" She got out of the cab and ran down the street back to her apartment. Terrified of losing her emotional control in public, she didn't leave her apartment for a week. A secretary, she called in sick with "a bad case of the flu"—afraid that she would have one of these breakdowns at work.

For Ron, grocery shopping was extremely painful. "I'd hit the frozen food section, take one look at the double chocolate chip ice cream—Jan's nightly craving when she was pregnant—and suddenly feel my whole body shake. My throat would tighten and my lips would start to quiver. I knew that if I didn't get out of the store as quickly as possible, I might start to break down. The first time I went shopping after we split up, I panicked and fled the store, leaving a full cart of groceries behind. Until I felt more in control, which really didn't happen until I was in the fourth stage of resignation, I hired a housekeeper who did my shopping once a week. It was tough on my budget, but the expense was well worth it. I needed someone who could handle the domestic details of my life."

Leslie found that she needed another suitcase to pack her things, after making the decision to leave Jack because of his cocaine habit. "Here we were, a nice suburban couple, with two kids in college, living ordinary lives, and he gets hooked on cocaine. When I came home from work and found him free-basing at the kitchen table, in a state of shock, I made the decision to leave.

I went upstairs and started throwing my clothes into suitcases, but I realized I needed one more. In my zombielike state I drove to the local discount store. I must have stood there for an hour, staring at all those suitcases, totally confused about which one would be best. Finally a salesperson approached me and when he said, 'May I help you?' I stuttered and couldn't remember what I came for. As I left the store, I was too disoriented even to be embarrassed and ended up driving to my girlfriend's house. I stayed with her for two weeks until I felt more focused and able to manage my emotions. I was terrified that at any given moment I might lose control. For the next couple of weeks I was able to get through work, and that was about it. As I began to feel more in control I started to do more things. But boy, in the beginning it was tough to get through."

While you're feeling emotionally overwrought, distraught, and out of control, it is wise not to add any extra stress to your life. Hire extra help, if affordable, to remove some of the burden. This is the time to call on family and friends for support. Take them up on lunch and dinner invitations. Let them help you out with your children or run an errand for you, if they offer. And ask them if you can call them when you are feeling lonely, afraid, or when you just need to talk, if they mind occasionally being your "911," or emergency number.

It may be difficult, especially while you are in grief, but make an effort to maintain any positive lifestyle habits you have already developed, such as an exercise program, meditation, or any relaxing hobbies that you enjoy. You'll find that exercise will help you release the feelings of frustration and anger that are prevalent during the third stage, setting blame. And if positive lifestyle habits aren't a part of your daily routine, try to incorporate them into your life now. Or if your routine has changed because of the breakup, make it your priority to form a new one that suits your present needs. A positive routine will provide structure where there is emotional chaos and help you move back into the mainstream of life.

Ron was very wise to hire a housekeeper to do the shopping and take over the chores that Jan always did. Leslie's girlfriend was a real lifesaver, giving her the moral support she needed as she tried to make sense of what had happened and how she could best get on with her life.

If you don't think that you can get through this period with just your personal support system, don't feel ashamed or become reclusive because you can't cope. Reach out and find the help you need from a qualified and ethical professional. If you find that you are suddenly suffering from headaches, stomach pains, or heart palpitations, see a physician for the appropriate guidance. Accept that during this period you may have occasionally to rely on antacids for your heartburn and tranquilizers for your "nerves"—but only under your physician's supervision.

For Marjorie, initially unable to function because of her grief, a "time out" week was the only way she could cope. Her physician also prescribed an anti-anxiety drug for her, which she used for a month, and sent her to me. While she was fortunate to be able to take a week off from work without being concerned that she might lose her job, this isn't always possible. You must be extremely self-protective against other losses at this time. To lose a job after losing love will only compound your fears and anxieties, so force yourself to function at work and maintain your regular routine to the best of your ability. You'll be surprised how losing yourself in your work or in a sport, activity, or hobby you enjoy will divert your attention, making you less fearful.

THE IMPORTANCE OF DIVERTERS

Before I discuss more of the common fears shared by most of my loveshock patients, I want to point out how useful *diverters* can be, during all stages of loveshock, in helping your to manage your fears. Basically a diverter is any constructive object or activity that you can focus your energy on—the very same energy that up until now you've invested in your love relationship. Just as an automobile needs shock absorbers to allow for a smoother ride over bumpy roads, when in loveshock you need a reserve of diverters to help absorb some of the emotional pain. And the more compelling the diverters are, the better they are, as they will command your attention in such a way that you will find yourself obsessing less and less on your loss and pain.

When Chuck and Darlene ended their fourteen-year marriage, they both wanted to stay in the house that they equally loved. Rather than going through a bitter legal battle, Darlene took the money from her settlement and decided to build her own house. While she couldn't afford anything too exotic, with the money she did have she was determined to design a house exactly as she wanted it. She became totally immersed in the project.

Building her house was such a compelling diverter that although Darlene was the rejectee, she traveled through her loveshock with less emotional pain than Chuck. She told me, "Every time I think I'm going to lose my mind, I remind myself that it is healthy that

I'm so in touch with my feelings. I also remind myself that my loveshock will end, and then I lose myself in planning another part of my house—whether it's the tiles for the bathroom floor or the kitchen wallpaper."

Douglas had always been what he called "a closet poet"—a traveling salesman with a love for lyrics. While he often submitted his work to agents and publishers, he had never had the satisfaction of being published. And his girlfriend, Brooke, did little to encourage him. In fact, she resented the time and energy he spent trying to get published. She constantly nagged him about using his time more realistically, and blamed his lack of promotion on his poetic obsession.

When Douglas and Brooke split up, he made getting published his top priority and it became his diverter. On the weekends, when he felt the pain of his loveshock the most, he concentrated on writing submission letters and investigating numerous magazines' guidelines for publishing. Nine months later a humor piece he wrote appeared in a local newspaper. This gave him the confidence he needed to continue. The last time we talked he was about to be published by *Reader's Digest.*

Unfortunately, many people don't realize the need for diverters in their lives until loveshock occurs. I have seen a tremendous amount of suffering in my older female patients, who have been living the traditional housewife role in which the husband and his needs come first. When divorce occurs these women are at a loss as to what to do with the rest of their lives. Those who have children, do charity work, and have created some outside interests cope better than those who have done nothing but focus on their mates. Their diverters give them something to hold on to as they work toward rebuilding their lives. Those women who have few or no diverters tend to be extremely slow travelers through loveshock, often becoming locked into the stages of grief and setting blame, and are prone to severe depression. To inspire them to take any sort of action to help themselves is difficult because they are often convinced that their lives no longer have any meaning.

When Greta came to see me, she had been stuck in the second stage of grief for a good six months. Her physician had referred her to me after he discovered that her chest pains were a symptom of her grief. After thirty years of marriage her husband had left her "to see the world" and had taken a blond ski instructor with him. Greta, who had come from Sweden with her husband when they were first married, had devoted her entire life to him. She had never been able to have children, which had always caused her great sadness, and now that Sven had left her she told me that she was ready to die. Greta was only fifty-five years old. She was pleasantly plump with a very sweet face. Her long gray hair was tightly braided and wrapped around her head.

As I asked her about herself she had very little to say. "Do you like to read?"

"No."

"Do you like to go to school?"

"No."

"Have you ever thought about getting a pet?"

"Well, I always wanted a bird, but Sven said no because he found them dirty."

"Yes, I understand. But Sven is no longer a part of your life, so why not treat yourself to a bird? It's time for you to focus on your wants and needs." As I watched her mull it over, a flicker of interest flashed across her face.

Two weeks later she had acquired a tame African

parrot whom she named Woody. He could talk a little bit, which enthralled her, and she began to teach him more. All the sweetness and love she had devoted to Sven she now gave to Woody. I was amazed not only at how intelligent Woody was, but at how quickly Greta was coming back to life.

Occasionally she would mention in our session, after Woody had mastered a new word or phrase, how clever her Woody was. Once when I called her she asked if I would like to speak to Woody. After we *all* had the following conversation I knew that she would be all right: "Here's what Woody has to say the next time Sven calls, Dr. Gullo." Suddenly I heard Woody's high, shrill voice squawk out, "Get lost, you jerk!" Greta's gusty laugh could be heard in the background.

FACING THE SILENCE OF ONENESS

While you are traveling through the stages of grief, setting blame, and resignation, you can expect a certain amount of fear and panic to overwhelm you as you confront living alone. For some of you, this may be the first time that you have ever lived alone. You went from living with your parents to living with your partner, so it's all the more challenging for you to adjust. Also, the longer you have lived with your mate, the more difficult you may find it to shift your lifestyle from togetherness to oneness. This readjusting and shifting, as you learn to live on your own, is what I call facing the silence of oneness.

Different patients interpret it in different ways, depending on how they are most affected. Marjorie called it "the screaming four walls" until she adjusted and decided that she liked the peace and quiet of her apartment after a long day at the office. However, it wasn't until she had reached the fifth stage of rebuilding that she made this adjustment. To Leslie it was "the empty bed syndrome," but after a few weeks she decided she'd rather sleep alone than with Jack, who was a restless sleeper because of his cocaine habit. Ron called it "TV dinners and boob tube time" until he began to motivate himself to cook some of the fresh food his housekeeper bought for him week after week.

When you first begin to live alone, it's natural to feel lonely and even to hate it. Your loneliness will probably be more profound on the weekends, late at night in bed, and during the holidays. Be patient with yourself. Adjusting to a new life experience always takes time and there are always setbacks.

So how do you cope; what can you do to counteract loneliness? Initially, during grief, when your loneliness and emotional pain are the most acute, do *anything* that makes you feel better—as long as it is not destructive to your well-being. Guard against excessive drinking, taking medications (except as prescribed by your physician), and any other negative lifestyle habits. When in doubt, it's best to abstain. Accept that the first few weeks, and maybe even months, will be difficult. Believe in yourself and know that you do have the strength to see yourself through.

If bedtime is particularly difficult, try taking a hot bath to relax. Sleep with the TV on or the radio playing, if the sound of voices comforts you. Ron chose to jog late every night, so that he would be too physically exhausted to care whether or not he was alone.

Concerned that there was something really psychologically wrong with her, Leslie admitted to me she was sleeping with her old childhood teddy bear. I reassured her that there was nothing wrong with her; in fact I congratulated her on being so resourceful.

Whatever constructive remedy works for you, use it. Don't worry about whether it's silly or not, getting hung up on the concept of what's normal and not normal. It takes enough self-control just to move yourself through the early stages of loveshock, remaining emotionally intact, without worrying about how normal you are.

Marjorie went through a period of insomnia, when she would sleep for a few hours and then find herself wide awake at 3:00 A.M., filled with fear of what tomorrow would bring. Rather than toss and turn in bed, she started to needlepoint. She kept the canvas and yarn by her bed and, when her insomnia hit, would turn on the light and immediately start working. Within half an hour she relaxed and found it easy to go back to sleep.

Coping with weekends will take some planning and real motivation on your part when your loveshock first begins. Do some traveling if you can afford it, go to the movies, or take a course. Try taking up a sport that you never thought you'd be good at and challenge yourself to do it. Do whatever it takes to divert yourself so that you do not start feeling sorry for yourself. Get involved!

Fill your free time with something meaningful. Greta became a volunteer at her local hospital, spending time with the sick children. She told them Swedish nursery rhymes, sang them songs, and even brought Woody to visit when the doctors would allow it.

In fact, one of the best ways to forget about your own suffering is to help someone else. And as you do, you will begin to realize your own strength, strength that will give you a renewed sense of confidence and self-esteem. Regardless of how weak and afraid you may feel, in helping others you are reminded that you are emotionally strong. This is why Earlene's work as a massage therapist was so effective in moving her through her loveshock. Although she was devastated to the point of suicide, her fears lessened each day as she gained confidence by realizing that she still had the ability to help others.

Holidays or once-shared events may be your toughest time—especially during the first year, and even if you are in rebuilding. It's difficult to feel happy and festive when you feel that you're all alone. Look to family and friends for support. Or treat yourself to a special trip.

While Jack eventually ended up in a rehab center, Leslie took her two children to Vermont during their Christmas break for a ski trip and had one of the best Christmases that she could remember. "I was amazed at how good and independent I felt. I realized that I didn't need Jack to have a meaningful Christmas. This trip also helped prepare me for resignation, for finally releasing my relationship with Jack. And the extra time and energy I gave the boys really brought us closer together. This has been a rough couple of months on them too."

YOUR POWERLESSNESS

Many people whom I have treated for loveshock have a hard time accepting that they are powerless over their situation and dealing with the fear that they have no control over the changes occurring in their lives. This is because they have spent the greater portion of their lives structuring situations so that they are in control. I encounter this problem most frequently in high-powered professionals and accomplished and attractive men and women. It's incomprehensible to them that they somehow can't buy, attract, or charm the relationship back into their lives.

No matter how much you have achieved, how successful you have become, or how attractive you are, you are powerless to hold on to a love relationship when it has ended. You can fantasize that it still exists, but the reality remains the same. And to continue with this fantasy, rather than dealing with the reality of your situation, only delays your progress through loveshock and may make it particularly difficult for you to get beyond the pivotal stage of resignation.

When Todd, scion of one of the greatest publishing families in the United States, came to see me, he was at once determined and confused. A man in his early forties, he was attractive, self-confident, and impeccably dressed. He had planned everything in his life, including the type of woman he would marry. When he met Barbara, an editor in chief of a popular's woman's magazine, he knew that she was perfect; he felt that their publishing careers beautifully complemented each other.

Initially he consulted with me not because he needed help with his feelings of despair or grief, but because he wanted to know what he should do to win her back. Barbara had left him three months earlier for a young writer who could barely pay the rent. Not only had she bought her own apartment, but she had moved the young writer in with her as well.

Todd refused to accept this, unable to imagine what in the world she could see in this struggling young would-be. Only fueling his frustration, he continued to send her flowers daily, had expensive gifts messengered to

her office on a weekly basis, and arranged for a chauf-
feured limousine to pick her up every evening after work.
The gifts were sent back, the flowers refused, and the
limousine left empty night after night. Barbara simply
wasn't interested anymore; all the power and the money
in the world couldn't get her back. Successful and self-
sufficient in her own right, her needs were far more
profound than what Todd had to offer.

As Todd talked, I felt as if I were taking part in a
boardroom meeting, deciding the fate of some merger
or big stock deal. Sitting back in the chair, with his arms
folded across his chest and legs crossed, one of the most
powerful men in publishing was looking to me for the
answers.

"You tell me, Dr. Gullo. You're the love expert. What
do I have to do to get her back? I'll do anything."

"You do nothing, Todd, except get on with your life
and release the fantasy. Accept the fact that your relationship is over and have faith that eventually someone
else will become a part of your life."

He looked at me with disbelief. "You're wrong. If
there is one thing that I have learned, it's that there is a
solution to every problem, that everything is resolva-
ble."

But I replied, "Barbara is not a business transaction.
She's a woman with needs that are now being met by
someone else. The sooner that you accept that you are
powerless over her decision, the easier it will get. You
can't make another person love you."

Todd left my office in a huff, totally dissatisfied with
my answer. I didn't hear from him for a month, until
one day he called me.

"Okay, Dr. Gullo, I've had it. Now what? I'm so
afraid to let go of the fantasy, but I'm such an emotional

wreck that I can't make sense out of anything anymore . . . This is so hard. I always win . . . I don't know
what to do . . ."

I proceeded to explain to him the stages and symptoms
of loveshock and that he was in the second stage of grief.
I reassured him that just as there is a beginning, there
would be, in time, an end. As he was finally able to
acknowledge that he was powerless over his situation,
his fear began to diminish and he began to move constructively through the stages of loveshock.

THE THERAPEUTIC ASPECTS OF YOUR FEAR

When you openly confront your fears, it's like taking
a long, hard look at yourself in the mirror. The flaws
become apparent. The fears that surface during the different stages of loveshock often indicate general vulnerabilities and weaknesses—your personal demons—
that you can correct.

As Marjorie worked through the anxiety of her loveshock, she realized that anxiety permeated all aspects of
her life. If she was unable to finish a report at work,
she'd stay awake that night worrying about getting to
work early the next day so that she could finish it. Two
weeks before her yearly physical she would become overly
anxious and convince herself that her doctor would
probably discover that she had some rare, incurable dis-
ease. She worried about everything. Her life was filled
with a series of *what ifs:* What if I lose my job? What if
I run out of money? What if I get in a car accident? What
if no one will ever love me again?

Regardless of what kind of love relationship she would
have in the future, she realized she needed to learn how

to control her anxiety; she understood how important it was that she focus on herself first and foremost. Everything else would eventually fall into place.

Marjorie learned how to meditate and began experimenting with different forms of relaxation therapies. She volunteered to work overtime at the office and used her additional income to join a health club and learn how to swim. But most important, she began to concentrate on focusing on the present—on enjoying and appreciating what was happening in the moment, not worrying about what the future would bring. As her fears decreased, her *what ifs* began to disappear.

It is painful to confront your personal demons. But when you do it, you become aware of how your loveshock experience can make it possible for you to grow and develop a stronger sense of yourself. A wonderful sense of self-mastery pervades you as you begin to take control over your life and manage the pain of your loveshock, instead of being consumed by your fears.

CHAPTER THREE

Rejector or Rejectee?

It is rare for two people mutually and simultaneously to decide to end a relationship. Usually, in a loveshock crisis, there are two roles to be played: rejector and rejectee.

While you might automatically assume that the typical loveshock victim is the rejectee, as I have worked with more and more loveshock patients I have seen that the rejector can suffer as intensely and experience just as many fears as the rejectee. In fact, the person who suffers more during the breakup is the person who is more significantly involved in the love relationship. That's because the one who is more involved has invested more time and energy in the relationship and ultimately loses a greater part of him- or herself.

THE REJECTOR: WILLING OR UNWILLING

I suppose if there is a "good" position to be in as a love relationship ends, it is that of *willing rejector*. When you are the willing rejector you have already divorced yourself emotionally and intellectually from the relationship, although you are still living with the other person. Perhaps this has been a slow process for you; perhaps you have gradually grown out of love with your mate as other aspects of your life have become more important and the love relationship has become a less important part of your life. You may even never have felt a profound love for the other person. When you finally choose to physically leave the relationship, you are acting out in your behavior what you have already resolved in your thoughts.

As a willing rejector you may feel an initial sadness that the relationship is not for you and will not last, but your traveling time through the stages of loveshock may be very fast. In fact, you may barely experience loveshock. By the time you actually end the relationship, you have already eased yourself through loveshock, weaning yourself bit by bit from the relationship until you feel comfortable in finally ending it.

Usually the most difficult aspect of the loveshock experience for the wiling rejector is a feeling of guilt if the other person refuses to accept that the relationship is over. Regardless of your emotional detachment from the relationship, it's difficult to watch your rejected mate suffer. Your greatest fear may be for his or her well-being.

This is what happened to Sharon when she decided to end her twenty-four-year marriage to Jeff. They had married when Sharon was eighteen and Jeff was twenty-five. She had just graduated from high school and Jeff managed a popular restaurant. While she couldn't afford to go to college, Sharon was eager to break away from her conservative, religious family. So when Jeff proposed, it was easy for Sharon to accept. After having three children in a six-year period, once the youngest was in school Sharon attended college part-time to get her degree. Juggling motherhood, wifehood, and scholastic demands wasn't easy, but she did it and in six years received her bachelor's degree. Jeff was in constant awe of Sharon's determination and ability to do it all. She went on to graduate school, received her master's degree in psychology, and became so wrapped up in the academic world that she decided to go for her Ph.D. By the time her youngest child was a freshman in college, Sharon was only forty-two, had become an assistant professor at the city college, and wanted out of her marriage. While she still loved Jeff, she was no longer in love with him and realized that the more she had grown as an individual, the farther she had grown away from him. They had little in common except for their children, who were now on their own. Unfortunately, Jeff loved and respected Sharon now more than ever. In fact, the more she accomplished, the more attractive he found her.

When Sharon consulted with me, she really came for Jeff, not for herself. Probably the strongest emotion she felt was guilt for causing him so much emotional pain. But the guilt she felt was not self-destructive, nor was it preventing her from getting on with her life. She had already found an apartment and was preparing to move out. The only thing stopping her was her fear of how Jeff would react when she finally left.

"Dr. Gullo, I can't live a lie. Even with my studies, I've always been a good wife and mother, but now that the kids are gone it just doesn't work anymore. I feel like I'm living with a stranger. I guess over the years I've just fallen out of love with him. But I don't know what to do. Jeff refuses to accept this split. He cries constantly and literally throws his arms around me and begs me not to go."

As she shared her story with me, she was calm and almost clinical. While she was genuinely concerned for Jeff's well-being, it was also clear to me that she was emotionally free of Jeff and that she was anxious to get on with her life. When she asked me, "What should I do?" I told her that there was nothing she could do. She was functioning well. She had faced a difficult decision and resolved it in her own mind. The problems and emotional pain were Jeff's, and only Jeff could work through them. The only constructive advice I could offer her was she suggest to Jeff that he see me so that I could help him get a grip on his emotions and understand what he was experiencing. But I stressed that it was a process that he would have to go through alone.

When you end the relationship as a willing rejector, you are already emotionally distant and probably somewhere in the final two stages of loveshock: rebuilding and resolution. At some point in the relationship you have already severed your emotional ties to the other person, probably as the final stage of a subtle, slow process that you may not have even been aware of. Then one day you chose to physically leave the relationship. Sharon was in the final stage of resolution when she told Jeff she was leaving: she was definitely ready to begin a new life cycle.

THE UNWILLING REJECTOR: VICTIM AND VILLAIN

Whereas the willing rejector suffers the least during the breakup and retains the most control, the *unwilling rejector* can experience as much emotional pain and trauma as the rejectee. Maybe even more, as you are at once victim and villain. Victim because you still love your partner, villain in that you must end the relationship—because the emotional pain it causes you is greater than any pleasure it may bring. This is a difficult dichotomy of feelings that you must work through.

The pain that causes you to push the other person away may stem from something as simple as your no longer feeling that you are appreciated or noticed—you're not getting the attention you need. In a sense you feel as though you have already been rejected, and you act out what you feel has already been done to you.

This was Denise's dilemma when she came to see me after leaving Cliff. A successful dermatologist, Cliff commuted back and forth between his Manhattan practice and his house in Connecticut. "I love him so much, Dr. Gullo, and I understand the strain of his busy practice combined with commuting, but he never seems to have an extra moment to spare. It seems that I spend my whole life waiting to be with him."

"What about the weekends? Do you take trips or maybe share a sport?"

"Sports—ugh! I'm so sick of baseball, football, and basketball that I could scream. Is there such a thing as a 'sportaholic'? If he's not glued to the TV he's in a stadium somewhere. Sometimes I'll go along just to be with him, but it's hard to feel close to someone when there are thousands of screaming people around you."

"Have you told him how you feel, made suggestions of things you'd like to do?"

"Dr. Gullo, I've tried everything to get his attention. One night, as he watched a Giants game, I sat down next to him on the couch in a black garter belt and black lace stockings."

"And?"

"And nothing else. Nothing happened! He merely patted my thigh while he continued to watch the game."

Denise was a good-looking redhead in her mid-thirties. I found it hard to believe that the combination of her long red hair and exotic lingerie couldn't entice Cliff. But from the look on her face as she bit her fingernails, I knew that her story was true.

"Every time I tell him that I need some attention, his stock answer is. 'What more do you want, Denise? You've got a beautiful home and clothes; you get to do whatever you want. But nothing is ever enough for you. I work hard to pay for all of this and I have to have my time to unwind. Sports help me unwind. Why can't you understand this?' "

"Do you think he's interested in another woman? I know it's not pleasant to think about, but could it be possible?"

"No! I don't mean to snap at you, Dr. Gullo—but I'm sure I'd know. I'm sure I'd sense *that*!"

"What about marriage counseling?" I asked.

"He refused. He told me it was my problem. So I moved out two months ago." Leaning on my desk, her head in her hands, Denise looked at me glumly. "What do I do? I love him and miss him so much."

"Have you thought about going back?"

"Go back to what? Even when he's *there,* he's not there. As much as I love him, I'm not happy—and I can never be happy!"

Whether it's something as basic as needing more attention, as it was for Denise, or something far more dramatic, like physical abuse, each situation is unique.

The degree of the problem that forces you to take this final action depends on your sensitivity and basic life principles.

What one person can deal with in a relationship may be unbearable for someone else. For example, one woman may not mind her husband engaging in extramarital affairs, if he is discreet. As long as she has a beautiful home, car, clothes, and the freedom to do as she pleases, she doesn't really care. She may even choose to engage in her own extramarital affairs—a fling with the tennis pro, the pool man, or even her husband's best friend. However, another woman may be tortured by her husband's infidelity, regardless of the material assets of the relationship.

This was the case with Julie and Brett. They shared three homes, two children, horses, and the country club life—a flurry of excitement and social activity. However, Julie found Brett's constant flirting at parties humiliating and demeaning. Rather than enjoying the luxury of her life, she lived in a perpetual state of mistrust and paranoia as she wondered if Brett was actually sleeping with any of the women he flirted with. They discussed his behavior and how it made her feel, but nothing changed. Finally, Julie refused to go to any social functions or parties with Brett. They argued constantly and Brett accused her of being crazy. Thinking that he might be right, Julie sought counseling. But when the therapist asked to see Brett too, he flatly refused.

While Julie, like Denise, had many material assets, emotionally she felt that she had very little. She told me that the happiest days of their relationship were when Brett was struggling to make it as a stockbroker on Wall Street. She didn't mind that a big night out consisted of pizza and cheap red wine by candlelight, because they shared time together, bonded their mutual desires and dreams. Now she merely felt like another one of his possessions. So, tortured by her mistrust, she decided to file for divorce.

Ironically, as the unwilling rejector, often you are not just fleeing a painful relationship but may be trying to save it as well. In fact, your rejection may be a cry for help. While you are saying, "You are causing me so much pain that I must end it," what you really mean is, "I want you to stop causing me so much pain so that I don't have to end it."

This was Matt's intention when he left Vicki because of her alcoholism. He loved her deeply, but he could not bear to watch her destroy herself. Forgotten appointments, embarrassing moments at restaurants, and disastrous dinner parties didn't help. But it was the evening he came home to find her passed out on the couch while dinner was burning on the stove that finally made him end their relationship.

As he later told me, "It was like one last slap in the face. All the past humiliation I had felt welled up inside of me and I thought I would explode. As I looked at her, disheveled and snoring on the couch while the potatoes burned on the stove, I felt a loathing for her that scared me. I wondered how I could at once loathe and love a woman so much. I had to get out."

Typical for the unwilling rejector, Matt was alternating between the stages of grief and setting blame when he came to see me. There was no doubt that he still loved Vicki, but he was angry that she had allowed alcohol to destroy their life together. One day he would rant and rave about her lack of self-discipline and unwillingness to deal with her problem, and a week later he would weep in my office because he missed her so much. Then he would blame himself for her drinking. The classic "If only I had done this or if only I had done that" was a constant refrain in his dialogue. And, as often is the case for an unwilling rejector, he began to think that he had overreacted to her problem. Eventually he convinced himself that he had made the wrong decision. His guilt and grief got the better of him, and a month after he had left Vicki he moved back in. But because nothing had changed and leaving her was the right decision, two months later he moved back out.

During this entire period he continued to see me, and there was no doubt that this man was going through his own personal hell. If ever there was an unwilling rejector, it was Matt.

The extreme zigzagging of actually reentering the relationship only to have to leave it again is often characteristic of the unwilling rejector. The emotional pain becomes torturous, the victim and villain within the unwilling rejector unreconciled and splitting the person in two. I constantly remind the unwilling rejector that behavior speaks louder than words: before you zigzag back into the relationship, make sure that there is real evidence of change.

Matt's loveshock took not only an emotional toll, but a physical one as well. He began to suffer from migraines, and his handsome, thirty-six-year-old face mirrored his internal pain as he broke out with patches of acne. It wasn't until he left Vicki the second time that he was finally able to move on to the goodbye stage, releasing her from his life as each day he was able to gain more emotional distance from her. As he became stronger, her pleas for him to return, with the promise of her change, became less effective. But it took him a year before he felt comfortable being on his own and was able to begin dating again.

During the rebuilding stage of your loveshock experience, you might reunite with your partner *if* he or she has changed the behavior that pushed you away. In fact, if there is a drastic change in the behavior, and both of you are willing to work on the relationship, you may be able to end loveshock at any stage. When behavior is corrected and the problems that split the relationship apart begin to disappear, you may be able to begin again because the dynamics of the relationship will have changed.

If both of you are willing, family counseling can be beneficial and can provide a strong foundation for what is really a new relationship. Had Vicki sincerely sought help and actually made the changes she continuously promised, I think that she and Matt might have had a chance to reconcile their relationship. This is how much he loved her.

However, I want to stress that family counseling and therapy are not magical cures. They will be beneficial only if both partners really want to work at the relationship. Truly, it takes two to make love work.

Often one person will go to therapy to assuage the other person's pain, hoping that it will help him or her accept that the relationship is over, or to ease guilt. And out of the couples that go to therapy, a large number still split up instead of staying together because therapy only clarifies whatever the reality of the relationship is. So when you go into therapy or marriage counseling in hope of repairing the relationship, realize that there are no guarantees. If, after all your efforts, the relationship still ends, you will at least have the satisfaction of knowing that you did your best to make it work.

THE REJECTEE: THE REAL VICTIM

As emotionally tumultuous as it is to be the unwilling rejector, the classic victim in the breakup of a love relationship is the rejectee. As the unwilling rejector you, too, may suffer, and you may have the added burden of guilt for ending the relationship, but you also have the advantage of being in control. Since you're initiating the breakup, you've had time to prepare yourself mentally, emotionally, and even financially for what you are about to do. But as the rejectee, you have no control over what is happening as your life is pulled out from under you. You are helpless as the impact of rejection throws you into a state of deep despair.

If there have been few or no indications of problems in the relationship, you will be shocked when you hear that the relationship may end. You will be in a state of numbness and disbelief. Regardless of the sensitivity and compassion the rejector may show in ending the relationship, you will still experience loveshock.

Alison broke the news to Seth that their marriage was over while they were dining with one of Seth's good friends. As they ate she turned to Seth and said, "I'm glad you brought Bert along because there's something I want to say tonight and I'm glad that he is here to give you some support." She continued, "Forgive the timing and the occasion, but I want a divorce."

Bert nearly choked, while Seth dropped his fork and turned white. This was the first inkling he had that anything was wrong in the marriage. He and Alison were both in their early fifties and they had settled into what he thought was a very comfortable, happy life. They traveled, played golf together on the weekends, and still made love at least once a week. Seth was in a state of shock for a good two weeks before he could even begin to comprehend emotionally what was happening.

When I took part in a panel discussion about men who had been left by their wives, a successful electrician, a member of the panel, was still in a state of disbelief that his wife had left him the month before. As far as he was concerned, he had done everything right to make their marriage work. He had always made an effort to be considerate of his wife's needs and had even willingly shared the household responsibilities, since both of them worked. He had even remembered the little things, often surprising her with little gifts or flowers for no special reason.

"One day, out of the blue, she came home from the hospital, where she is a lab technician, and announced that she wanted a divorce, because she felt that we had grown apart; she felt that she was no longer in love with me." The pain and perplexity etched in his face were so great that I thought he was going to break down in front of the audience. There was no response that I could give him, no conclusion I could draw except that at times it seems that for no apparent reason people fall out of love.

While your shock is the greatest when the rejection comes unexpectedly, as it did for Seth, even if you know that it is coming, the moment of rejection is still greater than anything you could have anticipated. It can still put you into a deep shock. To suddenly learn that you will no longer be able to see, talk to, or experience this person on the same intimate level is always psychologically overwhelming. Regardless of your awareness of the problems that have piled up, the differences and difficulties that have already pulled you apart, you can never be totally prepared for the emotional turmoil that follows rejection. This is why the initial onset of loveshock, especially the first two stages of shock and grief, are so devastating. Any intellectual ruminations and preparations you have made for this moment are like fire drills: they pale in comparison to the real thing.

FACING FAILURE

An additional problem you usually have to deal with when you are rejected, beyond your love loss, is the loss of a sense of self-worth. You experience a profound sense of failure and inadequacy. Rejection in any form is never easy, but when it is love that you have shared with another person and wish to continue to give that is being rejected, you are usually hit the hardest.

Your depression and hopelessness, most intense when you are in the second stage of grief, can diminish you so completely that you may find it difficult to function in any aspect of your life. When you are rejected you believe that you are unlovable and inadequate to everyone. Your feelings of inadequacy can permeate other areas of your life, and if they are not managed properly, your career may take a nosedive and your friends may disappear. Your loveshock will begin to snuff out your life.

As Seth told me, two months after Alison had moved out, "As to my feelings, Dr. Gullo, I truly feel as if my life is over. I don't know how to go on . . ." At this point he began to weep—a once sales executive crumbling in his grief. This second stage would take him several months to get through, and during it he lost many accounts and more than one friend.

It is not unusual for rejectors, especially unwilling

rejectors, also to feel as if they have failed. Their sense of failure and inadequacy stems from their inability to make the relationship work. Matt was convinced that he was a terrible failure because he couldn't get Vicki to stop drinking; for a while he shouldered the burden of her alcoholism. Denise was worried that she was incapable of sustaining a love relationship, since Cliff was her second husband. Julie felt that if she had been more exciting, maybe Brett's eyes wouldn't have wandered so much and she wouldn't have been forced to leave.

It's important, when this sense of failure and inadequacy engulfs you, to remember that you are responsible only for *your behavior* in a relationship and that you can't make the other person change his or her behavior unless he or she wants to. Your only concern should be the changes you need to make. This is why I constantly remind my loveshock patients that to sustain a love relationship requires a mutual commitment.

CHAPTER FOUR

Your Loveshock
Traveling Time

When Carolyn entered my office for her fifth session, I could see the rage churning inside her. Although she was impeccably dressed in a black silk dress, her eyes were full of fire. I had been seeing her every two weeks since her husband Bill had left her for another woman— a fact I found somewhat surprising, given Carolyn's good looks and wise, steady approach to life. However, I have learned in working with my loveshock patients that every story is unique and that there are always reasons for the breakup, regardless of how obscure they may be. However, in the earliest stages of loveshock, especially grief and setting blame, rather than delve into all the variables of the breakup, what's most important is to help people deal with their pain and move them through it at a rate that is at once healthy and respectful of their personal needs. A part of this is to recognize that people heal at different rates just as they grow at different rates.

"I'm furious, Dr. Gullo! Why won't they all just leave

me alone instead of constantly meddling and trying to fix me up? If I have one more strange man call me up and say, I know your good friend, such and such, and she suggested that I call you, I think I'll just hang up on him!"

"But Carolyn, doesn't it make you feel better to know that your friends care so much and want you to be happy?"

"If they cared so much they'd respect my need for privacy and leave me alone until I'm ready, or until I ask. My God, it's only been six months since Bill left me. I need this time to sort through it all."

"But would it be so terrible to have a dinner date or see a movie?" I was purposely playing devil's advocate to make sure that she was in touch with her true feelings."

"Not you too! Why can't anyone understand that I need this time to be on my own and become a whole person? After fifteen years of marriage, I don't want to risk even getting involved until I'm sure I'm ready. I can't stand the thought of ever having to go through this again. And I don't want to become one of those desperate middle-aged women who focuses her whole life on who will be the next date."

Carolyn's anger was healthy; she was reacting because her traveling time through loveshock was being violated. While her friends couldn't understand it, she simply wasn't ready to date.

Psychologists have long recognized the concept of *psychological readiness*. For instance, you may try to get a friend to stop smoking, a friend with a drinking problem to go to AA, or an obese friend or relative to go on a diet, begin an exercise program, or seek some sort of nutritional guidance. But until friends or relatives are ready to take the initial step on their own, all of your encouragement and support will amount to nothing. In fact, it may only alienate you from them as you make them angry by reminding them of something in their life that they're not yet prepared to confront.

Psychological readiness also applies to loveshock. If friends and relatives are urging you to leave one stage and travel to the next before you are ready, you may become resentful of their good intentions. But you should frequently evaluate where you are in your loveshock, referring to the description of the six stages in Chapter One, making sure that you are not stuck in a certain stage and locked in its accompanying behavior patterns. If you find that you are and are unable to motivate yourself out of it, then seek professional help.

Had Carolyn still been in deep grief, numb on Valium as when we first started working together, or even blaming herself for not being good enough to keep Bill faithful, I might have been concerned. But I was pleased with her progress: she was on the brink of taking that precarious step from setting blame to resignation. Soon she would finally be able to say goodbye, as she released a relationship that had been the focus of her life for fifteen years.

While Carolyn traveled through the stages of her loveshock, in many ways she was what I consider to be the *moderate traveler.* She did not get stuck in either passive or active response patterns. She wasn't spending evenings at home in bed with the covers pulled over her head, lost in seclusion. Carolyn wasn't locked in a state of grief, cut off from the world. Nor did she go out every night or find herself overindulging in food, drink, or men. In fact, she had begun working part-time for a suburban newspaper, honing journalism skills that had been her strength in college, and she continued her volunteer work at the local hospital two evenings a week that she had begun five years before.

As a moderate traveler, Carolyn recognized and accepted her pain as an inevitable part of the process of loss. She made every effort to deal with her feelings effectively and was not afraid to indulge in a good cry, from time to time, to release them. While she was anxious for the pain to end, she was able to accept that it would not end overnight. After all, her relationship had been fifteen years in the making, and it would take time to sever the bonds. While she was patient with her psychological healing process, she did her part too, actively seeking to diminish her pain through therapy and by keeping herself involved with new interests.

In touch with the reality of her pain, she dealt with it as positively as possible. Carolyn knew that holidays and certain events would be painful, so she planned ways in which to distract herself during these times. For instance, Christmas was a tough one for her, so she went to the Mideast with her college alumni group, and as she later told me, "lost myself in the wonders of Egypt."

Carolyn sought constructive support, not sympathy from her friends. This is why she was so offended when someone tried to fix her up with other men. It made her feel that she had no control over her life, that she was a helpless victim, when all she wanted to do was get through this painful period and take charge of what was left of her life. She had a need for emotional completion before moving on to another relationship, and for her a part of this process was her privacy. It was a little over a year before she went out on that first date, but when she did she was happy with the direction her new life had taken.

ARE YOU TRAVELING TOO FAST
OR TOO SLOWLY?

While Carolyn was moderate in her traveling time and traveled pretty smoothly through each stage, I don't want to play down the periods of deep emotional pain she experienced. However, she was able to manage her pain more effectively than would have been possible if she had traveled through the stages too fast or too slow. What was important for Carolyn and is important for anyone going through loveshock is to resolve emotional problems and personal issues that surface during a particular stage before proceeding to the next one.

However, I must warn you that this is not always a neat process. In fact, you can expect some problems that occurred in one stage to reappear in another. I actually had one patient who found herself still thinking about her first husband on the day that she was to marry someone else. While she loved her husband-to-be deeply, preparing for this wedding brought up tinges of sadness for the first marriage that had failed. I will discuss this zigzag effect in greater detail later in this chapter.

There is no ideal traveling time. But there is an ideal outcome of loveshock: to use the experience to grow emotionally and strengthen your capacity to relate and deal with loss in the future by overcoming personal vulnerabilities and major obstacles you meet while traveling through it. So the traveling time through loveshock varies in each individual, depending on the problems that emerge and the significance of the relationship that's ending.

One of the fortunate aspects of loveshock is that both your psyche and memory help you, gradually moving you through the stages. With time and effort on your part, your memory will block out your acute emotional pain, because if you had to live with the intensity and vivid memory of every hurt and loss that you have suffered in the course of your life, you would be unable to function. Your psyche has a natural tendency to move away from pain, seeking pleasure and equilibrium. When it is properly channeled through constructive activities, it will support your healing process. On many levels your emotional life is like your physical body. It too has a natural healing process that pushes you through your emotional pain if you don't resist it. Think of your emotional being as a psychological immune system, encouraging positive feelings as it attempts to block out what is negative and painful. Taking consolation in this, you should aim while traveling through the stages to flow with the pain while you allow your feelings to develop naturally, constantly reminding yourself that there is an end to loveshock.

Most of us deal with loss as we deal with life. If you typically run from stress situations in your life, you will be more apt to run from the pain of your love loss, traveling through the experience as quickly as possible and maybe even skipping stages. As a fast traveler you are so anxious to get beyond your pain that you learn little about the why of the breakup. You may continue to make mistakes in future relationships. Often your anxiety gets the better of you, causing you to become impulsively involved in behaviors and situations that may not be productive. You are also extremely prone to rebounding, throwing yourself into another relationship before you are ready. Eager to avoid the next wave of pain, you continuously jump from one thing to another at all levels of your life—ultimately accomplishing very little at all.

Palmer, a shrewd businessman, was good at juggling his numerous investments and loved manipulating his different financial interests. An upbeat man in his fifties, he preferred to avoid discussing anything unpleasant. Consequently, when problems began to surface in his marriage to Robin, who was twenty years younger, he kept a smile on his face and refused to acknowledge them. One day he came home to empty bureau drawers and closets: Robin had left him for another man, who, she explained in her note, "is kind, considerate, and always has time to listen."

Robin's abandonment hit Palmer hard. How could something like this happen to him? Instead of pausing, taking time to really look at the what and why of the failed relationship, he immersed himself in more business deals. As he later told me, "I decided it was time to diversify." His twelve-hour days became sixteen-hour days. His energy became frenetic and scattered. The only time he went home was to sleep. While his work in a sense became his compelling diverter, he took it to an extreme and consequently debilitated his health. He was terrified to relax because he was afraid of facing the fact that he was now alone. Six months later and nearly bankrupt, Palmer ended up in the hospital with what he thought was a heart attack. It turned out that his grabbing chest pains were manifestations of his anxiety and emotional turmoil: his loveshock was bound to surface somewhere. It wasn't until he was physically debilitated that he finally accepted that he would have to confront his emotional pain and go through his loveshock. And it would take patience and serious introspection on his part before it would go away. He would have to slow down and take a long, hard look at his life.

One of the most important things that the fast traveler needs to realize is that the pain of loveshock is an important part of the healing process. Do not be impatient with your psyche or try to ignore the pain. You can put it off by trying to race around it, like Palmer, but it cannot be avoided. Sooner or later you must confront and experience your love loss so that it can be released. Do not deny the pain of your love loss. It only delays the inevitable realization and, even worse, gives you a false sense of hope as you think you've reached rebuilding and even resolution, when in fact you haven't effectively completed resignation, emotional releasing of the relationship.

Whereas a fast traveler flees from pain, if you are a slow traveler, you tend to focus on your pain to the point of obsession. You may spend great periods of time reliving different aspects of the relationship and the pain of the breakup. While it's healthy for you to confront and play out your feelings, when taken to extremes the process may leave you stuck in the second and third stages of grief and setting blame. Passive in your response patterns, you may find yourself frozen with fear of what will come next. In a sense you are caught in your own personal time warp, as you move through each stage in agonizing steps. Getting to the point of resignation and actually moving through it, saying goodbye to what once was, can be overwhelming. It's as if you don't want to let go of the pain because to do so is to let go of a past that has meant so much to you.

Lindsey's loveshock overwhelmed her life to such an extreme that she was unable to hold a job. An attractive, bright, twenty-two-year-old secretary, she had fallen in love with her boss and was thrilled when he responded to her flirtation. While they were making wild, passionate love several nights a week, he was also making wild promises that he never intended to keep. Victor took her with him when he traveled, reassuring her that as soon as the time was right he would leave his wife. Whenever she expressed her doubts, he bought her a love gift to pacify her. Three years after the affair began, Victor sadly said farewell to Lindsey because his wife was suspicious.

But for Lindscy, saying farewell seemed impossible. Besides all the gifts, she had kept a postcard from every hotel they had ever stayed in and matches from every restaurant they had dined in. She also had ticket stubs from every movie they had ever seen together: Victor had become her whole life.

After ending their affair, he had found her a good job with another company, thinking that it would be inappropriate if she stayed on as his secretary. While the job was challenging and she should have been enjoying the tremendous salary increase, all she could think about was Victor: the candlelight baths they had shared, the intimate dinners, the cozy movies. With Victor, even a car ride was exciting. She relived the memories over and over again. Six months later she was still turning down dates and spending her evenings with her memorabilia. Eventually she lost her job and found herself drifting from one occupation to the next; her only motivation was to pay the rent.

Instead of constructively traveling through her loveshock, she was perpetuating her role as victim. Locked in the second stage of grief, she finally sought counseling when she ended up at the state unemployment bureau, standing in line for five hours, waiting to sign for a check.

You must guard against positioning yourself as victim, as Lindsey did. If you think you are a victim, you are more likely to respond to your loveshock crisis passively. Locked in the memory of what was and in the pain of what is, you often think that your life is no longer your own. In a sense it isn't, because your behavior defeats you as you resist your psyche's natural inclination to flow through the stages. You can't imagine how you'll go on with your life, so you purposely stop dead in your tracks. Your own resistance to traveling through the stages becomes a roadblock to your emotional well-being.

EVALUATING YOUR TRAVELING TIME

While the general profiles above can provide you with a good indication of whether you are a fast or slow traveler or a moderate traveler like Carolyn, you can probably identify in some way with all three. However, it is the predominance of any one pattern that will determine your traveling time through loveshock.

The following chart, which lists *general* characteristics of the fast, moderate, and slow traveler, is one way to further evaluate your traveling time. It will also make you aware of specific behaviors that may be operating in extremes and distorting your traveling time.

For each number, circle only one characteristic that best describes your behavior. Once you've completed the test, add up your total in each column. The column with the greatest total indicates your traveling time through loveshock.

Fast	Moderate	Slow
1. anxious during conflict	realistic during conflict	depressed during conflict
2. denies emotional pain, *avoids*	faces emotional pain, *confronts*	is overwhelmed by emotional pain, *retreats*
3. tries to do several things at once	finishes one task before going on to the next, methodical	lacks motivation or finds self-motivation difficult
4. makes hasty decisions	weighs decisions carefully	has difficulty making decisions
5. is uncomfortable with discussion or expression of feelings	deals with feelings openly and releases them	obsesses on feelings
6. blames others and situations	shares responsibility for blame when appropriate	feels confused about what went wrong, where to place blame
7. needs to control others, situations, feelings	focuses on self-growth first	needs to be nurtured by another, sees self as victim

8. extroverted	flexible, depending on the situation, adaptable	introverted, lacking confidence
9. has had more than one loveshock experience	has had at least one loveshock experience	has had little loveshock experience
10. overachiever, is never happy with what is	achieves realistic goals	underachiever, or is easily diverted from goals

Again, the speed at which you are traveling through loveshock is not the overriding issue. But certain characteristics of the fast and slow traveler can impair your recovery. If you were fast or slow for numbers 1 through 6, be aware that moderating these behaviors can help you move through your loveshock experience in a more complete and less painful way.

Remember that as a fast traveler your greatest obstacle to recovery is your avoidance and impatience with the pain, as well as the tendency to deny that your loveshock even exists. Remember Palmer? It wasn't until he ended up in a hospital that he acknowledged his loveshock. As a slow traveler your greatest obstacle to recovery is your dwelling too long in any or all of the stages. Look what happened to Lindsey because she couldn't move beyond her grief: she ended up unemployed and essentially nonfunctioning.

Whether you travel too slow or too fast, your goal should be to confront your emotional pain realistically and to allow your psyche to move you through each stage at a rate that is appropriate for you. It's how well you deal with the critical issues that come up at each stage that's important, not whether you are a fast or slow traveler. Ultimately, I discover what is best for my patients by observing what enhances or impedes their ability to function. In terms of your own love-shock, if you can say yes to the following questions— regardless of your pain—you are traveling at a rate that is right for you:

The Traveling Time Self-Test

- Are you accepting and dealing with your loveshock as you continue to function in your daily routines? (Are you getting to work on time, paying your bills, maintaining your personal appearance, taking care of your health, keeping appointments?)

- Are you learning from your loveshock things about yourself and your personal needs? (Perhaps you are discovering that you need to develop friendships and work on other family relationships. Also, your love-shock may make apparent personal needs that were not being fulfilled in your past relationship. Ideally, these needs will be fulfilled in a future relationship.)

- Are you gaining from your loveshock something that will ultimately enrich your life—not just the pain? (Maybe it is something as basic as a better understanding of yourself and your own strength or sensitivity. Or perhaps, as you've looked for ways to fill the void, you've developed a new skill or hobby, advanced in your career, or begun an exercise program.)

THE ZIGZAG EFFECT

Whether you are a fast, moderate, or slow traveler through loveshock, a critical dimension of your traveling time is what I call *the zigzag effect*. To zigzag is to spend a considerable amount of time traveling back and forth among the different stages.

In the early stages of loveshock, until you complete stage four, resignation, this is to be expected. One of the most common zigzags is to go back and forth between grief and setting blame. Remember Matt, the unwilling rejector of his alcoholic wife, Vicki? As he was working his way through loveshock, he would get beyond his grief, finally setting blame as he vented his anger that she had allowed alcohol to destroy their love. Instead of moving on to resignation, two weeks later he would zigzag back into grief, weeping in my office because he missed her so much. Zigzagging between grief and setting blame may go on continuously until you are ready to resign yourself to the reality that the relationship is over.

However, it is not uncommon, although it is painful, to complete resignation and actually be in rebuilding when suddenly you have an overwhelming desire to reconnect with the other person. While your intellect may know better, your heart pulls you back into the past. You may actually zigzag all the way back into grief. But if you really have completed resignation, this zigzag will be brief and the emotional pain will not be as intense as when you were actually traveling through the grief stage. The same is true if you zigzag back into setting blame: your anger will be of shorter duration and not as intense.

Remember the loveshock patient who found herself

thinking about her first husband on the day she was to marry someone else? She was actually in the final stage of resolution, starting a new life with another man, and up popped the memories of her previous marriage.

When Valerie called me after her honeymoon with Grant she said, "I know that my loveshock is over—in fact it has been for some time—but the strangest thing happened on my wedding day. I had just put on my peach silk wedding dress and was adjusting it, looking at myself in the mirror, when suddenly I started thinking about Hugh. And for a brief moment, as I looked in the mirror, I went back fifteen years in time and saw myself dressed all in white. My father was smiling at me: he took my hand and led me into the chapel . . ."

There was silence on the line and I waited for a moment. "Valerie?"

"Yes?"

I could tell by her voice that she was caught up in the memory again. "Are you all right?"

"Oh! I'm sorry, Dr. Gullo—I'm fine. I was just realizing that the brief sadness I felt then I don't feel at all as I tell you about it. I guess I just had a momentary zigzag. How silly of me!" She proceeded to tell me excitedly about her honeymoon in Acapulco.

Had Valerie not started talking about Acapulco, I would have told her that her brief zigzag was not at all silly but very normal. While your emotions during loveshock may follow a predictable course, at times they seem to have a mind of their own. It's not unusual for a piece of the past to suddenly haunt you when you least expect it.

As time passes and you continue to travel through your loveshock experience, the number of zigzags that you have will decrease. And each time you do zigzag you should find it to be a little less painful. As one patient put it, eight months into his loveshock experience after the end of a nine-year relationship, "Now if I zigzag, it's only a momentary twinge."

LOVESHOCK FLASHBACKS

Often a zigzag is set off by what one of my patients appropriately labeled a "loveshock flashback": a place, a person, an event, or a thing that reminds you of a special moment in the relationship or just brings up the memory of the other person. A song, passing by a restaurant that you once shared, or even a piece of clothing can trigger a loveshock flashback.

For Nancy, who had progressed to rebuilding, every time she opened her drawer and looked at the beautiful lingerie Gene had bought her when their affair first began, she had a loveshock flashback. Even though she knew that he was a married man, she fell deeply in love with Gene as the affair progressed. After two years, still in love but tired of being the other woman, she ended the relationship. The beautiful lingerie brought up such vivid memories that she had to throw it away. "I couldn't even give it away, because then it would still exist, somewhere, and so would the memory of him and all those exquisite moments we shared."

While it's fairly simple to get rid of things or avoid places that trigger loveshock flashbacks, holidays can present another problem. Also in rebuilding, Lloyd found it extremely difficult to deal with Mother's Day. When I answered his emergency call he was in a state of total despair, recalling how he and Liz had opened their house in Nantucket for the summer every Mother's Day during the previous five years. Suddenly he found himself yearning for her presence on all levels: the perfume she wore, the clam bakes they had shared, and her presence in bed. At that moment, even the thought of her weight problems didn't bother him. He couldn't believe his emotional tailspin, especially since he had started dating again and felt that he was finally over Liz. I reassured him that his feelings were perfectly normal and that during the first year following a breakup—regardless of where you are in your loveshock experience—holidays and special occasions could be emotionally draining. Because they have a special impact on your psyche, it takes more time to put emotional distance between yourself and these occasions.

CYCLES OF LOVESHOCK

There are also what I call the *cycles of loveshock,* which create a structure for zigzagging and loveshock flashbacks. I have found that most of my patients, even those who have had a minimal amount of emotional pain, have to travel through a full year following the breakup before they are free of zigzagging and loveshock flashbacks. I have also observed that as you approach the final season at the end of your year, you may once again focus on all that you have lost. And even though you have come so far, perhaps even to the final stage of resolution, the pain can be gut-wrenching.

James and Candace had ended their relationship the previous autumn. I hadn't had a session with Candace since July, when suddenly, at the end of October, she scheduled an appointment. As she stood by the window in my office, watching the leaves blow off the maple trees, tears began to stream down her face.

"I was doing so well—and now this. It's like I'm back there in it. I don't understand. I know that I was at the end of my loveshock, and now I feel like it's beginning all over again. I'm starting to think that loveshock is some horrible cancer that goes into remission for a while but never really goes away. When, Dr. Gullo, when? When will the pain really end?"

"Exactly what is going through your mind at this time? Where is your focus?"

"I keep thinking about the day he came to get his things. How I had to leave the house because I couldn't stand watching him put his life in boxes. And when I came home I felt so empty. His closets, his drawers—there was nothing in them. I can vividly remember going through the house, one room after another, and then suddenly realizing that we would never share any of it again."

"Do you remember what you did after you realized this?"

"Yes. I stood in front of the big picture window and wept as I watched the leaves blow and fall from the trees in the front yard. I was terrified, convinced that my life was over. I felt like I was withering up inside and dying . . . just like the leaves."

"Do you feel terrified now? Do you feel as if your life is over?"

Slowly she recouped, blowing her nose and blotting her eyes. "Why no. As a matter of fact, I'm busier than ever before. I just finished a course on astrology, something I've always been interested in, and a group of us from the class are going on a retreat to a holistic center in Vermont. However, I am convinced that there is a real man shortage; except there is this one guy from my class that I find rather intriguing . . ." She was laughing, her pain dissolving.

I explained to Candace that her sudden grief had simply been triggered by the season and that in reality she was at the end of her loveshock experience. I also reassured her that by the following autumn, while she might still have the memory, there would be little or no pain associated with it.

Time is your true friend when you are a loveshock victim. Each day that passes provides more emotional distance, the pain diminishing bit by bit, as you travel through the stages to an end that will arrive.

CHAPTER FIVE

Love Pitfalls: The Five Most Common Loveshock Mistakes

There are certain *love pitfalls* that you are vulnerable to during loveshock, usually during the stages of grief, setting blame, resignation, or rebuilding. These love pitfalls are destructive behavior patterns that you act out in reaction to your love loss. It is not unusual to experience more than one pitfall during your loveshock experience. You may go through different ones during different stages or experience two or three at the same time.

Recognize these pitfalls, rather than recoiling from them. Most of us fall into at least one pitfall during a loveshock experience. But there are strategies you can employ to work your way out of all of them.

The five pitfalls, which I describe in this chapter, are: *hanging on, rebounding, moth-to-flaming, escaping through excess,* and *comparison shopping.*

HANGING ON

When you're *hanging on*, you don't want to let go of the relationship mentally, emotionally, or physically. A slow traveler through loveshock, you are clinging to whatever you hope or think is left of the relationship. But in your refusal to let go, you are only prolonging the inevitable—confronting the fact that the relationship is over. Hanging on is acted out in three different ways, each of which hinders your traveling time through loveshock:

Obsessional Thinking

This can be torturous. You spend many hours thinking about your ex-mate, unable to focus on your own life. A prisoner of your obsessive thoughts, you cannot escape from the other person. He or she invades your dreams and can even alter your behavior.

You may find yourself arranging "accidental" meetings, constantly phoning the other person, or sending passionate letters of remorse. Night and day you are consumed by thoughts of what the other person is doing: Where is this person now? Who is this person dating? At what restaurant? Where is this person spending the weekend?

Samantha found herself reacting in all of these ways during the first two months of her loveshock. A former model and presently the owner of a little boutique, she was proud of how far she had come since her modeling days. "The fashion world thought that I was nothing more than a dumb blonde. What a surprise they had when I turned my love for fashion into a successful business."

When her ten-year marriage to Maurice ended because of his prolonged affair with a young model, obsessional thinking overwhelmed her. Instead of focusing on her lucrative business, Samantha spent numerous hours reliving her past with Maurice. In her thoughts, she remembered only the good times. As she lost herself in fantasy, her business began to suffer, and when Samantha went to bed at night she experienced sleep disturbances as well. As she told me during one of our first sessions, "Oh, Dr. Gullo, the torment of my Maurice, my lost love, haunts me and threads itself through all of my dreams. There is no escape."

If you're an obsessional thinker during loveshock, you too may toss and turn, sleeping restlessly, or wake up after eight hours and feel as if you have not slept at all. The anxiety that you are consciously experiencing invades your subconscious as well. Like Samantha, many of my patients complain about the persistent torment of their obsession.

Often you zigzag back and forth between the second and third stages of grief and setting blame. Songs, movies, particular places, and certain foods can trigger your emotions: first the longing to share a particular moment with the other person again, and then intense anger with yourself or the other person as you try to set blame. Even worse is the profound emptiness you feel, and the nagging doubt of "Will I ever find another?"

Regardless of the intensity of your obsessional thoughts, with time they will burn out. Until they do, try this *thought-blocking technique:* Every time you start thinking about your ex, adamantly say to yourself, *"STOP!"* Then begin thinking about another topic that's equally compelling, or engage in an activity that will divert your focus. Again, diverters are important; seek out new interests that really grip you. The key here is to block out thoughts of the other person by substitution. Don't expect immediate results. However, I promise that the more you practice this thought-blocking technique, the more effective it becomes.

Samantha found the thought-blocking technique difficult at first because a part of her was reluctant to let go of her obsession with Maurice. She diverted herself with the specific goal of discovering a new designer. I also had her make up note cards to place by her telephones, at home and at her boutique, that said in bold writing, *"STOP! DON'T CALL!"* As her obsession naturally faded, bit by bit, her self-respect also returned, because she knew that she had taken an active part in regaining emotional control of her life.

Revenge Loving

You are particularly prone to this pitfall if you are the rejectee. Hurt by the rejection you have experienced, not only do you involve yourself in another relationship before you are ready, but its dynamics evolve from your anger. You may act out your revenge loving in three different relationships styles:

First, you may involve yourself in another relationship (your new partner becomes the third party) strictly with the intention of making your former partner jealous. Desperate for attention, you arrange to meet up with your old love so that he/she can see how easy it is for you to find someone new. Often, the third party is hurt the most, aware too late, when already emotionally involved, that he or she is just being used.

Second, you may involve yourself in another relationship and then subconsciously act out on another person what you feel has been done to you. For example, if your ex abused you, you may find yourself abusive to your new partner. Or if your ex manipulated you, you may—determined never to be manipulated by another person again—become very manipulative of your new partner.

Or third, you may enter into a relationship where you feel that you can be totally in control, so that no one will ever have the power to hurt you again. Ultimately you become bored, restless, and angry with the other person who allows you to control him or her; in the end you find yourself unhappy and hurt.

After Lynn left him, Bruce immediately became involved with Louise, who was a waitress at the local restaurant where he and Lynn often dined. Because he knew Lynn's habits, Bruce usually entered the restaurant when she was there and made a point of showing not only Lynn, but everyone in the restaurant, just how friendly he and Louise were. So hurt by Lynn's rejection, Bruce was determined to hurt her and show her how desirable he still was. Fortunately Louise ended their relationship before she got hurt because she was aware of Bruce's true intentions: to get back at Lynn. Eventually, Bruce also realized that he had developed his relationship with Louise strictly out of vengeance. His was a classic case of revenge loving.

Gordon's wife, Yvonne, had also left him, but his revenge loving pattern was more complicated. When Gordon came to see me, I was in awe of the level his anger had reached. While he had been profoundly in love with her, she had only cared about him because of his wealth. Once she had taken all that she wanted, she simply packed up and left while he was away on a business trip. Within the six-month period since she had moved out, he had actually been with a different woman every weekend—and with each woman he subconsciously acted out the same style of abuse Yvonne had inflicted on him.

During the week, he would cruise the different Manhattan nightclubs until he found the "weekend woman" of his choice. Before the weekend he would send her flowers and a note promising a real relationship. What an enticement for any woman: good-looking, charming, independently wealthy, and only in his late thirties. It would be easy to believe that he was a real-life Prince Charming.

On Friday night he would pick his weekend woman up in his red Mercedes sports coupe and whisk her out to the Hamptons for the weekend, leading her to believe that she would be the next mistress of his house. Unfortunately for the woman involved, as the weekend unfolded, it was just one party after another and a lot of meaningless sex—but no true emotional contact with Gordon. Each Sunday night, after he had taken what he had wanted, he left the weekend woman at her front door with barely a civil goodbye.

When I asked him to tell me about some of the different weekend women he had been with in the last month, he could barely even remember their names, let alone what they did or any interests they might have shared with him. He was so lost in his anger and caught up in his revenge loving pattern that he had become completely disconnected from any emotional intimacy. His anger made it impossible for him to love.

In order to move yourself out of a revenge loving pattern, first realize that it is a natural reaction when you have been rejected. You need to recognize your anger and release it. The healthiest way to do this is to act it out within yourself, not with another person as Gordon repeatedly did.

Many of my patients have found that keeping a diary or journal of all their feelings (one method of self-monitoring) is extremely beneficial in working their way out of this pitfall. Gordon started doing this and found that he was able to write much of his anger out, experiencing a great sense of relief, as he became more in touch with how he felt and why he was feeling it. Just admitting that he was filled with anger was a big step for him. I knew that because his case was so extreme it would take a great deal of therapy before he could have a real relationship again.

Correspond with your feelings, through your journal, twice a day—even if it's only a few lines. In the morning describe what you're feeling in general, as you begin another day, and in the evening evaluate your reaction to different people and situations that you dealt with during the day. You may want to spend a considerable amount of time once a week writing out any hurt or anger you are still feeling. And if you have begun any other relationships, honestly evaluate your real feelings and the role these relationships are playing in your life. Many of my patients have found this form of self-monitoring invaluable in helping them understand and deal with their anger.

If you feel that you are unable to cope with your anger and find yourself going in and out of different revenge loving relationships, like Gordon, consult a therapist or counselor. You may need some additional guidance to get you back on track and to help you become more objective about your feelings. When you are able to objectify your feelings, the anger and the hurt begin to dissolve.

Magnifying

When you've been rejected, it's not unusual to magnify what you *think* your ex is doing. You are convinced that he/she must be having a great time living it up while you are brokenhearted. If magnification is your way of holding on to the lost relationship, you spend a great deal of time moping about in your grief. As your world seems to have grown smaller, you become convinced that his/hers has grown larger. At the core of your magnification is your own self-pity that here you are with nothing left while the other person has everything.

Teddy was convinced that Rosemary was going out every night, enjoying her new-found freedom, while he was struggling to put his new apartment together. He felt anything but motivated as he came home after work to "rooms of emptiness." Why hang a picture or a plant? Why paper the bathroom—what was the point? Surrounded by his self-created nothingness, night after night he collapsed into bed in a heap of despair. His life had no meaning. All he could focus on was what Rosemary was "probably" doing at any given moment. He would take long walks, filled with thoughts of Rosemary and the wonderful time she *must* be having. Rosemary had wanted the divorce, and for all he knew she was basking somewhere in the Mediterranean sun with a Greek lover.

Much to his surprise, a month after we started our sessions, he ran into her in a coffee shop where she was having dinner and reading the newspaper—totally alone. She was wearing no makeup and looked as if she had put on about ten pounds. Teddy seemed incredulous as he told me, "She's the one that wanted this, but she looks more miserable than me!" He began to realize how irrational his magnification was and how it was preventing him from progressing through his loveshock.

There is a natural tendency in some of us to enjoy
our own sorrow. I've seen it in many of my loveshock
patients. If you allow it, magnification can become a
kind of martyrdom. You must be careful that you don't
use it to avoid focusing on your own needs—things that
you could be doing for yourself to move yourself away
from your pain.

While you may be in loveshock because of the actions
of another person, how you handle it is your responsibility. Again you must motivate yourself to do things,
incorporate different diverters into your life that will
take you out of yourself. Don't waste another day thinking about how miserable you are. As one of my patients
so aptly put it, "Yes, I have to deal with the reality of
my situation: I was dumped. But I can also tune out
and stay in motion."

The thought-blocking technique used to redirect your
obsessional thinking is also helpful in moving you through
magnification. Every time you start magnifying the other
person's life, adamantly say to yourself, "STOP!" (repeating several times if necessary) and engross yourself
in a pleasurable activity. Terry would continuously repeat "STOP!" to herself the moment her magnification
of Clint began, and would continue to do so as she took
herself to a movie, play, art opening, or concert. Once
there, she would lose herself in the performance. "I
replaced Clint with the arts. After a while it became
apparent to me what a waste of time it was to magnify
his life, when I could be filling my life with so much
culture."

Also sit down and make a list of every positive aspect
of your life. This might include things like good health,

a good job, good looks, good family relationships, close friends, a nice home, a nice car, or a healthy bank balance. Tape this list to your bathroom mirror and every time you start feeling sorry for yourself, stare at yourself in the mirror as you read your list out loud, beginning "I have . . . " and going down your list. You will find this form of positive programming very effective in moving yourself out of your self-pity.

Another aspect of magnification is idealization, constantly focusing on all the wonderful qualities of the person who has just rejected you. While your natural tendency to block out pain and to preserve what's positive and pleasurable in your life is vital in easing you through emotional trauma, it can also make it more difficult for you to separate yourself from the other person.

This happens most frequently during the setting blame stage. I recommend that whenever you find yourself only focusing on the positive aspects of the other person, sit down and make a list of every negative thing that you can think of. Do this often and you will find yourself becoming much more objective, as you begin to see the relationship for what it really was. Your idealization will lessen and you will be able to focus your attention on getting on with your life.

REBOUNDING

The opposite of hanging on, *rebounding* is a pitfall typical of fast travelers who fill their lives up with numerous activities to avoid their emotional pain. Whereas in hanging on, you need to motivate yourself through loveshock, when you're in rebounding, you need to slow yourself down so that you can effectively master each stage of your loveshock before moving on to the next one.

In rebounding, you find it difficult to stay in at night, just to read a good book or watch television. It is as though you just can't sit still. And spending a weekend alone can drive you right up the wall. So you escape loveshock through a whirlwind of one-night stands or by entering into a new relationahip prematurely, before you have reached the resolution of your loveshock. This premature relationship quickly burns itself out, only adding more trauma to your shaky emotional state. This was true for Gabrielle.

Gabrielle and Paul married because Gabrielle was pregnant. A year later, while he adored his young son, Paul unfortunately couldn't sustain the marriage because he just didn't love Gabrielle. After he moved out, Gabrielle was in such emotional pain that she was unable to properly care for her son. Her mother volunteered to look after him and suggested that she just get away from it all: perhaps a trip to the Caribbean or Mexico would do the trick, easing her heartache.

Choosing a secluded hideaway in Mexico, Gabrielle felt sure that the sun, sand, and sea were just what she needed. But she also hungered for something to fill the emotional void created by Paul's rejection. So rather than working through her pain alone, allowing herself just to relax in the beauty of Mexico and sort out her feelings, she quickly became involved with a man, also staying at the hotel, who showed her warmth and kindness.

She later told me that a few days after they met they went to bed and when they made love, she closed her eyes and fantasized that she was with Paul. When she awoke the following morning, finding this stranger beside her, she was filled with such anxiety and dread that she packed her bags and fled Mexico that afternoon.

Fortunately Gabrielle didn't continue this behavior, but often after one rebound you move on to another, regardless of your trauma. You continue to fill your life up with meaningless relationships because you can't bear to face your emotional pain or to be alone. Facing the silence of oneness, as discussed in Chapter Two, is one of your greatest fears. But as you run from one relationship to the next, your hurt and fear are still with you, unresolved.

Every time you think that you are "falling in love," you are really "falling in need." Rather than confronting your pain, you cloak it within the structure of another relationship. The dynamic is "I love you because I need you." What you're really looking for is a psychiatrist or baby-sitter, not an equal partner.

While Gordon's behavior was a form of revenge loving, as he abused his weekend women as his wife had abused him, he was also rebounding—going from woman to woman, weekend after weekend. Weekends meant playtime, and he couldn't bear to spend any time alone.

Continuous rebounding is particularly common among men because they have a greater difficulty than women in dealing openly with feelings and confronting emotional pain. In fact, some of the most severe cases of loveshock I have seen have been in men. As they go from one woman to the next, each conquest temporarily rebuilds their ego. But eventually even the thrill of the conquest becomes boring, providing less and less pleasure and making the man realize that he must meet his emotional pain, head on, once and for all.

In order to overcome this pitfall, you first need to

recognize what you're doing; acknowledge that your life has become frenetic and that your rebounding stems from your pain as well as your general inability to be alone. The next step is to gradually recondition your behavior so that you become comfortable with being alone.

Initially you may want to try alternating one night at home with one night out, working toward spending an even greater number of nights at home. For your evenings at home, plan some sort of activity that will make the evening pleasurable. At first, you may not be able to spend your evenings at home alone: this might be too radical a change and only intensify your pain. Invite someone over whom you enjoy being with. Or give a dinner party. This is a good time to cultivate new friends and call on old ones.

But eventually you are going to have to make yourself tough it out alone. Chances are you won't have a very good time, and you may feel a bit of panic at first. This is the time to have a new book on hand, to rent some new movies, or to work on a special project that you have been putting off. You may find yourself fidgety and on edge, pacing the rooms and unable to concentrate. Several of my patients have resolved this uneasy state by taking long, leisurely baths and listening to soothing music. Others report that some easy yoga exercises and some good deep breathing while saying to themselves, "I am calm," over and over again helps to ease the anxiety.

Whatever reactions you have, remember that pain is to be expected in the beginning, as you adjust to your aloneness. Know that every night you manage to stay home alone, you will become stronger and more self-assured and develop greater self-awareness. And in time, as you become at ease with yourself, the reasons for the breakup will become clearer to you.

One of the unique aspects of psychological growth is that when you force yourself to do something that makes you feel emotionally uncomfortable but that you know will ultimately benefit you, you start feeling better about yourself because you are taking control of your emotions, instead of allowing your emotions to control you. And as you gain more control over your emotions, your pain begins to diminish because you are mastering it. Remember that pain can be constructive; the challenge is to function to your best ability as you deal with it. Often the most self-destructive thing you can do is to continue to run away from your pain.

MOTH-TO-FLAMING

This is one of the most painful pitfalls of all, as you actually act out your obsessional thinking, and a form of zigzagging, as you are constantly drawn back into your old relationship only to be hurt over and over again. You are like a moth drawn to a flame. And just as the closer the moth gets to the flame, the more it's hurt, the more you subject yourself to the other person's continuous rejection, the more you suffer. It is your compulsion to constantly try to re-create the relationship, regardless of the humiliating rejection that makes this pitfall so devastating.

Although rejected, you continuously beg to be taken back and constantly look for ways to reintegrate yourself into the other person's life. You may find yourself constantly telephoning him/her, leaving presents, sending notes. All of your actions only reinforce your denial that the relationship is over.

Far from impressing the other person, this lavish attention is likely to be an annoyance. And as he/she reacts with continual rejection and indifference, you are subjected to further pain, feeling even more diminished as your self-esteem sinks lower. Just as the flame destroys the moth, repeated rejection destroys you.

In the grip of obsessional thinking over Maurice, Samantha was also moth-to-flaming in her attempts to entice Maurice back into her life. She would go out of her way to bump into him at his favorite nightclubs and restaurants—first spending hours making up and dressing up, hoping to seduce him back. She would leave impassioned messages on his answering machine and then sit up most of the night waiting for him to return her call, which he never did. She even sent him a rare orchid with a note: "Our love will never die, as it is as rare as this orchid."

The more Samantha obsessed and played it out, the more Maurice rejected her. But so blinded by the light of the flame, she continued in her attempts to get closer. However, Maurice became so annoyed by her obsessive and moth-to-flaming behavior that he got an unlisted telephone number and stopped going to his old hangouts.

While her impassioned telephone messages and the gift of the rare orchid helped her imagine that she was somehow once again a part of his life, in reality she was being ignored. It was her persistent compulsion to keep trying, regardless of his constant rejection, that made her realize she needed help. Samantha had reached her emotional bottom, for she had lost all sense of the reality that the relationship no longer existed. Later, as she regained her emotional control, she told me, "I thought I was worthless without him. I felt depleted and powerless. And the more he rejected me, the more I wanted him. It was as though he had become an addiction—he was my fix—and I didn't know how I could live without him."

In severe cases of moth-to-flaming, it is not until you've reached your lowest emotional level, like Samantha, that you finally realize that you cannot make someone else feel something that they don't feel. Not all the gifts, phone calls, or begging in the world is ever going to make the other person give what they cannot give.

If this is your pattern, what you must focus on is stopping any actions on your part that are going to subject you to further rejection. Again, as with obsessional thinking, this means taking action: leaving yourself a note on every phone not to call, applying the thought-blocking technique of saying *"STOP!"* every time you are tempted to reinvolve yourself with the other person, and filling your life with diverters to take your focus off the other person.

I've also had patients make a tape for themselves about the dynamics of the relationship: what was good about it, when and why it began to change, why it had to end, and in what ways it was beneficial to them that it did end. Making a tape helps you understand the difference between what once was and what now is. Whenever you are tempted to call or do anything that will draw you back into the relationship, listen to the tape. Hearing your own voice telling you the truth over and over again will make it easier for you to maintain your self-control. (I will give you more information about making a love-shock tape in Chapter Seven.)

Often we become self-deluded about the reality of our

relationships because we simply can't bear the pain that we associate with the final letting go. The denial can overwhelm us. We'd rather keep singeing our wings, fluttering closer to that flame, than fly away alone.

If the other person continues to act kindly toward you and even agrees to see you from time to time, you are going to have to do a reality check. Don't confuse kindness with love: the other person may initially respond favorably to your actions simply out of respect for you and your former relationship, without having any intention of ever coming back.

Time spent with someone you have broken up with may leave you with unrealistic expectations as you think, "Oh, gosh, this person really misses me, wants to come back to me." Now is the time for total self-honesty on your part, as you ask yourself these questions:

- Was your time together romantic, or are you creating something that wasn't really there?
- Did this person voluntarily make physical contact with you, or did you force it?
- Was there true tenderness and a real show of feelings, or are you seeing in the other person's behavior reactions that aren't really there?

If you are convinced that there is still some flicker of interest, a small chance that the relationship can be rekindled, ask the other person to think about your relationship for a week or two. Ask him/her to call you back. Nine out of ten times he/she never calls back; if anything, he/she is relieved to be let off the hook.

Taking this step, saying, "I'll leave it up to you, all right?" will take a lot of courage on your part. If he/she does not respond as you hope, your self-respect is still intact because you have allowed the other person to make the choice. Once again you are taking control over your life, moving yourself through loveshock, and ultimately doing what's good for you—instead of acting out of desperation for some momentary relief.

ESCAPING THROUGH EXCESS

Unfortunately, one of the most frequent responses to loss and rejection is compulsive behavior, or what I call *escaping through excess*. This is a pitfall that is easy to succumb to because without the other person you feel that your life is no longer balanced. As the scale is already tipped, it is easy to slide into excess.

The most serious form of excess is drug and alcohol abuse, using either or both to numb your pain and compensate you for your love loss. The problem with these substances is that since they only provide temporary, short-term relief, you may turn to them repeatedly to prolong your relief. In doing this, instead of regaining emotional control, you only lose more control. When full-blown, escaping through excess is the most dangerous love pitfall of all. That's why during loveshock it's important that you consider yourself in a high-risk period, and if anything be overly protective with yourself, avoiding all addictive substances. I have counseled many drug addicts who began their flight into addiction because a serious love relationship ended and alcoholics who began their heavy drinking as a way to numb the pain of divorce. You hear examples of this pitfall in the news every day, and you can probably think of cases among your own friends.

If this is your pitfall, you are denying a basic reality

of life: that what provides momentary pleasure and relief cannot provide you with any real happiness or solutions to your emotional problems. Seeking happiness through any of these excesses will only end up being destructive. I guarantee you that attempting to escape through excess while coping with loveshock is a no-win situation that can lead to permanent physical and psychological damage.

If you find yourself falling into this pitfall, do not tolerate it. Accept the fact that you need help. Be on your guard against your denial, which may lead you to think, "I can handle this. I've got it under control." This type of denial will only involve you more deeply, as you are literally digging your own grave.

Realize that the reason that you are escaping through excess is that you cannot handle your emotional pain; you really are out of control. Nobody engages in self-destructive behavior when they're in control of their lives.

I cannot stress enough how important it is that you take action immediately and seek professional help, whether it be through therapy, counseling, or one of the twelve-step self-help programs that are available. There is an anonymous self-help group available for almost every substance abuse problem that exists, including Alcoholics Anonymous, Narcotics Anonymous, and Cocaine Anonymous, to name just a few. If you have any confusion about how and where to get help, a community health professional (or, of course, your personal physician) will be able to point you in the right direction.

Perhaps not as destructive and dangerous, but also physically and psycologically damaging, is compulsive eating. While food may keep you company during those lonely loveshock nights, confronting the extra pounds when the worst of your loveshock is over will just be another psychological setback that you'll have to deal with as you rebuild your life. Beyond your appearance, sudden and excessive weight gain can contribute to health problems such as high blood pressure.

If you're prone to diving into a box of chocolates night after night rather than dealing with your feelings, I recommend that you carefully monitor your food intake. Know that for every unneccessary morsel you indulge in, ultimately there is a price to pay in pounds and inches, and maybe even with your health.

When Marlene started her therapy, she had gained five pounds in the two-week period since she and Bobby had split up. This was not difficult to do, since she worked in a delicatessen. A pretty woman in her twenties, with black hair and blue eyes, she told me that dieting had always been her demon. "It seems as though I've spent my whole life starving to remain a size ten. But I love food—cooking it, eating it and selling it. And since Bobby and I split up, I just don't care anymore. What the hell—why not eat the cheesecake? I can down a pint of ice cream and not even think twice about it!"

But the fact that she was in my office, seeking help, indicated that she really did care. The last thing she wanted was to come out of her loveshock a size fourteen. She also had a family history of diabetes. I advised her to keep a food diary. Before she ate anything she had to write down what it was she was about to eat and what her emotions were at that moment. The diary not only made her aware of all that she was eating, but provided her with some insight into how she was using food as a substitute for the love that was no longer a part of her life.

To control her snack attacks at home, I had her buy an exercise bicycle and place it in the kitchen. When she got the urge to snack, it was up to her to get on the bike and pedal for as long as it took for her to regain her self-control. When working at the delicatessen, I urged her to reach for raw vegetables instead of potato salad.

While I provided the therapy, it was up to Marlene to follow through with her own self-discipline. A month later, although still zigzagging between setting blame and resignation, Marlene had lost the five pounds and was ecstatic with her new thigh muscles.

COMPARISON SHOPPING

You feel that you are ready to date, but unfortunately no one meets up to your expectations because you are constantly comparing anyone that you meet to your ex. If comparison shopping is your pitfall, it usually takes one of two forms: either you are looking for someone who is just like your ex, or you refuse to consider anyone who has any similarities to your ex. You may fantasize what I call *the model of perfection,* as you create in your mind an unrealistic idealization of what a partner should be like. Anyone that you meet is bound to fall short of your expectations because there is no perfect person.

When you are looking for someone who is a clone of your ex, it may be because you still have not completely accepted your love loss and may be still experiencing some obsessional thinking. You're hoping to find an identical replacement. Conversely, if you dismiss anyone who reminds you in any way of your ex, it may be because you're afraid to experience the same emotional pain.

Either way, you're operating in extremes—but this is one pitfall that's fairly easy to correct. You have to get in touch with your needs and also to understand that regardless of how much you have been hurt, you stayed with your ex for perhaps several years because he/she did fulfill certain needs within you. The secret is to find someone who fulfills your needs without the hurt or incompatibilities involved in your previous relationship. So focus on your personal needs and how they can be met, and do not allow yourself to compare a new acquaintance to your ex. You must consider any new people that you meet as individuals.

I had one patient, a well-known actress, who had already been through three marriages when she came to see me. She had one of the most extreme cases of comparison shopping that I had ever counseled.

Each marriage had ended in similar unhappy circumstances, and as she contemplated taking the plunge for the fourth time, she became concerned. She didn't want to make another mistake. During the course of her therapy she realized that since her first marriage she had rebounded from one unhappy marriage to the next, never completing the stages of loveshock after any of the marriages had ended. And each time she rebounded, it was into the arms of another man who was similar to her first husband.

Brad had been the real love of her life—an exciting, sexy man who also had a bad gambling habit. So with the good things that made her happy, the bad came as well; she continued to attach herself to men who were slick. She thrived on the excitement. But unfortunately, with the excitement came the gambling. And whether it was because of risky business deals or the roulette wheel, ultimately each husband would rely on her for the money. In the end the business deal would fall through or Lady Luck would flee, and she was left with nothing but a smaller bank balance.

Concerned that her fourth marriage would disintegrate like the previous three, I had her make a list of her personal needs and what was important to her in a relationship. "Excitement" was at the top of the list, but so was "not to be used." What she needed to realize was that there were plenty of exciting men, exciting men who were independent and did not need to rely on her money or celebrity status to feed their excitement. Until she made this list, she had never stopped to think that by being selective, it was possible to have the excitement she craved without the risks.

As she analyzed her list and took a close look at the history and character of her current love, she made the decision to hold off on the marriage. A month later she called me, and I could hear a real sadness in her voice. "Jordan's gone. He left a week ago because I wouldn't back his latest venture. I think from now on, Dr. Gullo, I'm going to take it a lot slower. Comparison shopping is not for me, and I've got to stop rebounding. It's time that I face my emotional pain once and for all . . . ."

When a love relationship ends, your emotional foundation—badly shaken—usually cracks where it is the weakest. Think of any love pitfalls you experience during loveshock as the cracks. Know that you can patch and smooth out these cracks strengthening your overall character.

Overcoming the love pitfalls is another of life's challenges, providing you with the opportunity to become emotionally stronger. As you work your way out of, over, and beyond the pitfalls, you will be left with an enhanced sense of self-worth and self-esteem. You will realize that *you* are capable of fortifying your emotional foundation, that *you* have the power to curb and maintain your emotional self-control.

CHAPTER SIX

Resignation: Saying Goodbye to Love

Lorna sat in my office with two rather large boxes next to her. The combination of her bright blue cashmere dress and medium-length white hair was stunning. In the six months that we had been working together, her physical transformation had been amazing. When she had first consulted with me she had been rather frumpy and nondescript-looking: the emotional pain had overwhelmed the person.

Initially Lorna had been in a passive response pattern, cutting herself off from everyone and everything in her grief—including the people who could divert the misery that had engulfed her since Andy had ended their thirty-year marriage. During our earliest sessions, when Andy had just moved out of their house and into his girlfriend's apartment, she would come to my office and for the first half hour of our hour session weep and claim that she must have failed miserably for this to happen to her. At times she would become hysterical, so full of rage that she secreamed at me, "What did I do to deserve this? I did everything I could to please him. Oh God, what are the kids going to think of me when they find out?"

Lorna dreaded telling her son and daughter about the breakup because she was convinced that they wouldn't understand and would blame her. Since her son was in the Navy and her daughter lived in Oregon, physical contact with either one of them was infrequent. But they were very close, keeping in touch through photos, tapes, and letters. Eventually they would realize that something had happened. I encouraged her to tell them before Andy did, stressing that while they might not understand at first, they would surely continuc to love her as they always had.

Finally, a week later, she called her daughter from my office and explained to her as calmly as possible what had happened. As her daughter responded, Lorna began to cry. The conversation ended as Lorna quietly uttered into the receiver, tears running down her cheeks, "Nothing . . . Nothing . . . I'll call you soon."

As I handed her a tissue, I feared the worst. However, while she was still crying, her eyes were shining. "I can hardly believe it, Dr. Gullo. Do you know what she said? She said that I was terrific. She said that I was good and strong and the best mother anyone could ever have. She wanted to know if she could do anything for me. And the last thing she said was, 'Mom, I love you, no matter what.' "

She took the next step and wrote her son. He responded immediately, via radio from his ship, with concern and understanding.

From that point on, Lorna began to fight back and

actively deal with her loveshock. To fill the long hours of aloneness, she took a part-time job in a department store. Much to her surprise, she met other women at work, divorced and widowed, who had managed to rebuild their lives. They served as role models as Lorna realized that there was more to life than marriage. Her children's love was also an important incentive. Because her daughter's input had been so positive, I suggested that she call her on a biweekly basis for a boost of confidence to get her through the early stages of grief and setting blame.

It was hard work for Lorna to leave her self-pity and self-blame behind. And she struggled out of more than one pitfall: obsessive thinking, magnification, and compulsive eating were her personal demons. Ironically, her attractiveness and self-confidence blossomed as she worked her way through the pain. These qualities were, in a sense, the rewards of her loveshock.

But Lorna hadn't completed her loveshock yet. She was in resignation, what I also call the goodbye stage—the pivotal stage of every loveshock experience and for many, the worst part of loveshock.

Resignation is the most crucial stage of your loveshock experience; it is the time when you make the decision to release the relationship from your life once and for all. It is your time to say a final goodbye to what once was and will never be again, as you realize that you can no longer spend your life yearning for what might have been.

Lorna was at once desperate to let go and unable to let go. This is the major obstacle that all loveshock victims must get beyond in resignation before they can travel on to rebuilding, and why Lorna was sitting in my office with two large boxes full of everything that was portable that reminded her of her past with Andy. She found it too difficult to let go and get through her resignation on her own.

We were about to begin the *linking objects exercise,* in which she would get rid of any articles that evoked negative feelings, while keeping those that still affected her positively. And as much as she wanted to say goodbye and get on with her life, she was hesitant even to begin this exercise. This was not unusual; I had experienced this with other loveshock patients.

WHY YOU MUST LET GO

Long after love ends it may still linger in your thoughts, influencing your present and future behavior. While you are no longer in the relationship in reality, you are still married or emotionally attached in your mind. This is why completing resignation, the fourth stage of loveshock, is so important. Until you do, you are unable to continue traveling forward because you just can't let go, and you can't travel back to the past because your partner is no longer interested. Your life is on hold until you come to terms with your loss.

In fact, until you withdraw your emotional energy from the other person, you can date a hundred different people but none will ever please you because you are still married or committed elsewhere in your mind. It is imposible to get on with your life. If you are in loveshock and you want to know how long the pain will go on, I can tell you that it will last as long as you permit the relationship to exist in your thoughts. It will be difficult for you to let go and emotionally detach from the other person. But it is your responsibility to determine when you want to stop feeling the pain and take that final step of saying goodbye.

Choosing whether you should consider the other person as a friend or never even speak to him or her again may be hard. I have found that most of my patients who remain in contact during a divorce or breakup seem to have more emotional pain and often find it all the more difficult to let go. Sometimes, they find it necessary to have several *last meetings* before they can let go. The choice is yours, but I think that it is very important that you evaluate your feelings, and consider how you may feel afterwards, before you make contact with the other person.

There may, however, be practical considerations that make contact unavoidable, such as an amicable divorce settlement, shared business interests, or joint custody of the children. If these contacts with your ex-mate diminish you in any way or leave you feeling emotionally distraught, let your lawyer handle *everything*. You may have to sever your business connections. This is especially important if your partner has been cruel or abusive to you.

Unfortunately, many who should don't have the luxury of severing all ties because of joint custody of their children. If this is your situation, you may want to have a friend with you for support during those times when you must make contact with your spouse, for instance when he or she is picking up or dropping off your children. The discomfort you intially experience will begin to fade, once you have finally released the relationship.

WHY IT'S SO DIFFICULT TO SAY GOODBYE

While you know and remind yourself, "All I have to do is remove the other person from my thoughts," you still feel and have to deal with the realiity that you are losing a significant part of your life. And the longer the relationship lasted, the more difficult it is to accept that it is over. One of the most common statements I hear—in fact, I can't think of one loveshock patient who has come out of a long-term relationship who didn't bring it up—is, "I've invested so much time—all of those years. Where do I go from here? Is it worth it to start all over again?"

When a long-term relationship ends, you're not just losing the other person, you're losing an entire history. And you can expect to suffer multiple losses as well: your social network, your in-laws, and often your home, your lifestyle, your pet, and favorite possessions. Besides the love, you are losing a whole chunk of your life that existed within the context of the relationship. That is what makes it so hard to say that final, necessary goodbye.

What I tell my patients at this point is, "Yes, a part of your life is over. And you may feel, at this moment, that it was the best part that will ever be. But, in time, you will find that you will be able to build something in place of it that will be as rewarding and enriching as what you have lost."

Lorna compared traveling through resignation to walking through a long, dark tunnel filled with everything from the love relationship: "As you walk by it all, toward the light at the end of the tunnel, you must say goodbye as you keep walking. Your heart aches and you want to cry. And you want to stop and embrace each memory, each person and each thing one last time. But you realize the longer you linger and hold on, the longer you stay in the dark. So the trick is to keep walking, not to stop, because if you keep walking you will eventually have said goodbye to everything and be in the light. Once you are in the light, you can see clearly. You have regained your perspective of what is real and what is fantasy." The analogy is a good one; resignation isn't the destination, it's only a vital step to get you over your pain. Your life doesn't stop when you say goodbye in the darkness: it's about to begin again in the light.

I would add to Lorna's analogy that when you are walking through this unknown, dark tunnel, it's normal to stumble along the way. If you do, all that matters is that you get up and continue to move forward. Although you may be fearful, push yourself along. And take with you, from this journey, those things that give you comfort and will continue to enrich your life in the future—as you move on to rebuilding.

THE FINAL ACT OF SAYING GOODBYE

Because it is so difficult to say goodbye, to let go of an important love relationship, I have found an active therapy of actually acting out resignation to be very effective in getting my patients over this last major hurdle of loveshock. There are three parts to this therapy: the personal statement, confronting what went wrong in the relationship and why it ended, and the linking objects exercise.

First, it is important that you make a *personal statement* of what you saw in the other person, what attracted you to become involved with him or her, and what were the positive and negative aspects of the relationship. By doing this you acknowledge that you got involved with this person by *your own choice*. This process will also help remove any vestiges of magnification; you will cease to idealize the other person and the relationship.

You can either make a cassette of this personal statement or write it out. Do what you feel has the most impact on you. Some of my patients do both. Whichever method you choose, make sure that you begin and end your personal statement with "This relationship is over. X is no longer a part of my life. The sooner I let go, the happier I will be."

Lorna had been keeping a diary of her feelings since the beginning of her loveshock, so she chose to write her personal statement out: "This relationship is over. Andy is no longer a part of my life. The sooner I let go, the happier I will be. I was attracted to Andy the first time I watched him play football in college. He was a wonderful athlete—so strong and yet so graceful. And he did all the right things when we dated. He was the perfect beau. There were lots of flowers and he never pressed himself on me. He was a real gentleman. When he went to Korea and became a captain, I knew that I'd marry him if he came back alive.

"Andy was hardworking and always pushed himself a little more so that we could have more. We were one of the first couples in our apartment complex to have two cars, and I remember how proud he was when we moved into our first house. We took wonderful vacations because he liked adventures. But he was short-tempered and didn't have patience when it came to dealing with the kids. This is embarrassing to write, but he never really satisfied me sexually. In fact, I never really thought that he cared that much about sex: that's why I was so shocked that he left me for a girlfriend and still am. When he said, 'I do,' I thought he meant it. But now I know that he was with his girlfriend for two years before he left me. I married one man and ended up being married to someone else. This relationship is over. Andy is no longer a part of my life. The sooner I let go, the happier I will be.''

The second important part of this therapy is to *clearly confront what went wrong in the relationship and why it ended.* Your personal statement will help you connect with this. After reading Lorna's, I asked her what her conclusion was.

Her response: "The man who left me for another woman was not the man I married. I don't feel that I have to blame myself for failing in this marriage. He changed, I changed—our changes took us in different directions."

And then I asked the key question, which would ultimately help her make peace with herself and release any guilt she was feeling: "What responsibility, if any, do you take for this relationship ending?"

Lorna looked away as she answered, "Well, I got pretty wrapped up in the kids and all of their activites. There were plenty of times when Andy needed to vent his frustrations or just talk about what was going on at work. I wasn't a very good listener: I was so involved answering the children's needs, I had no time to listen to Andy . . . I also let my physical appearance go. I know now how important it is to always look the best that you can. It shows the other person that you care not just about him, but about yourself as well."

Many of my male patients tell me that once the children came along, their wives stopped working on their relationships, and at times they felt extremely neglected.

This was where Lorna had been at fault, and felt she had to take partial responsibility for Andy's infidelity.

All of these realizations were bringing Lorna closer to letting go. She was finally able to step outside of the relationship and evaluate it objectively and even learn from her pain. Rather than thinking in terms of "failure," she had begun to think in terms of "different"— that Andy's needs were different and the dynamics of the relationship could not fulfill these needs. This is why he left.

If you have been in the role of rejectee, and the other person said, "I don't love you anymore," what he or she may really have meant was "My needs have changed and I no longer love what you have to offer me." Don't think of yourself as a failure or inadequate because of this. Realize that just as the other person needs to find someone else who is better suited to his or her needs, so do you. By the time you reach the final stage of resolution you will be in touch with your needs, aware of what it takes in a relationship to make you happy. Many of my loveshock patients have ended up finding someone better suited to them and are much happier today, in their present relationship, than they ever were in their previous relationship. Wisdom in love often follows loveshock.

Having taken responsibility for your part in the ending of the relationship, you must release yourself from the burden of being perfect. Lack of perfection, a characteristic we all share, is one of the major reasons we beat ourselves up psychologically. Instead, give yourself permission to make mistakes, and realize that working through them is what allows you to grow. Your objectivity in recognizing your needs and realizing your right to satisfy them, as well as acknowledging your responsibility for what has happened, will help you move on to the rebuilding stage of loveshock.

THE LINKING OBJECTS EXERCISE

Having made her personal statement and having clearly confronted what went wrong in the relationship and why it ended, it was the right time for Lorna to begin the *linking objects exercise*. As she began to take out snapshots, cards, jewelry, and a couple of pieces of clothing, she looked at me painfully and asked, "Why do I have to go through this?"

"I know that this is painful, but it is a necessary step in coming to terms with your love loss. All of these items were a part of a relationship that *was* an important part of your life; these are a part of your personal history. By remembering the positive and negative feelings associated with each article, you will be confronting your personal pain and will become less frightened of it. This exercise also allows you to release the energy of the other person once and for all, as you get rid of any articles that you feel still draw you back into thoughts of the relationship. And any articles that evoke negative feelings you should give away or throw away. It is also important that you identify any *unrealistic* romantic fantasies associated with each item. These fantasies could be preventing you from releasing the relationship."

Before Lorna began to go over each article that she had placed on my desk, I reminded her of the early days of her loveshock; I reminded her how far she had come. "Remember how you used to spy on Andy, watching him enter his girlfriend's apartment building from the pay phone across the street?"

She looked at me, shocked. "Oh lord! I was so obsessive! I really did some stupid things, didn't I? And what about my fake suicide attempt? I tried everything to get his attention. What a waste of time!"

"While this may be the worst experience you have ever been through in your life, Lorna, one look in the mirror will show you how well you have come through it all, how you have grown from your pain. You've progressed so far, it's time that you let the rest of it go. And as you do so, realize that you are also letting go of all the mistrust you once felt, the fear of not knowing where Andy was, and your feelings of betrayal."

"I know," she said. "You're right—let's get on with it. Okay. All the jewelry has to go. Andy always gave me a piece of jewelry for our anniversary. It's meaningless now."

"Perhaps your daughter might like it."

"That's a thought. And if she doesn't want it, I'll sell it—except for this . . ." Lorna held a gold charm bracelet with two tiny charms in her hand. I could see the tears in her eyes. She cleared her throat and continued, "Ah, he gave this to me when Tracy was born and added the second charm to it when Jimmy was born. This I'll keep and maybe even wear, because two wonderful kids did come out of that marriage."

As she went through the rest of her things, discussing what each one meant to her, there were more tears. But there was acceptance as well. She finally decided that except for a family portrait and the charm bracelet, everything she had brought with her had to go; these were the only things she felt strongly about in a positive way. The clothing would go to charity, the jewelry would go to her daughter or would be sold, and the photos, cards, and other bits of memorabilia she actually dumped in my wastebasket. "This way, I won't be tempted to retrieve them!"

While the linking objects exercise is extremely effective in moving you through resignation, helping you to resolve your feelings so that you can finally let go, it can also be painful. Your goal should be to integrate what you now see as the positive parts of your history into your new life while you remove the relationship itself from your thoughts. One patient said that when he did this exercise he felt the same grief and longing he had felt when he packed up his mother's possessions after she had died.

You may want to do this exercise with a friend, family member, minister, or therapist for support. And timing is also important: while it's natural to resist saying this final goodbye, don't force yourself to do it if you really don't feel that you are ready to handle it. If you have any doubt about what you are selling, giving away, or throwing away, ask a friend to store these items for you until you are sure. Or put them in a safety deposit box or vault. The point is to remove them from your daily contact. I had one patient who sold a valuable Oriental vase, only to learn a year later that it was worth far more than what she was paid for it.

If you decide to do the linking objects exercise alone, do it on a day when you are feeling good about yourself and the direction your life is taking. It's a lot easier to let go of the emotions that keep you locked in the past when you believe in your future. It's also helpful if you have an uplifting and positive activity planned for afterwards: a meal with good friends, a funny movie, a massage, or a shopping expedition. This will reinforce in your mind that your life is moving forward in a positive direction, that you have finally come to terms with the *what was* and *what is* of the relationship that has ended. As you complete this exercise, know that you have just taken a big step into your future.

Lorna had two wonderful children that would continue to be a part of her life no matter what. She also had a beautiful house that she loved and felt very secure in, regardless of whether or not Andy shared it with her.

Here is how some of the other people I've mentioned earlier in the book acted out the linking objects exercise:

Earlene got rid of all the records she and Ed used to dance to.

Nancy threw away the beautiful, sexy lingerie that Gene had given her and then replaced it with equally beautiful lingerie in a different color.

Lloyd sold the summer house in Nantucket that he and Liz had shared and bought himself a little fishing cabin in Maine, something he had always wanted.

While her closest girlfriend held her hand, Lindsey burned the postcards, matchbooks, and ticket stubs that she had collected during her romance with Victor.

Palmer gave the expensive designer bedding from his king-size bed to his maid. "Once I changed the bedding, I could read in bed at night without constantly being distracted by thoughts of Robin."

Remember Seth, whose wife, Alison, announced that she wanted a divorce while they were dining with their friend Bert? After he did the linking objects exercise, Seth decided to trade his car in for a new one because whenever he glanced at the passenger side, for a brief moment the image of Alison flashed through his mind. "It was as though I was seeing a ghost!"

The conclusion Seth came to, as he traveled through resignation and on to rebuilding, was, "This is my reality. I can go on being miserable or I can accept that this has come to an end. This means letting all thoughts of my ex-wife go. I am now free and ready to begin again. I'm on my own now. Whatever I'm going to have in my life is what I'm going to create for myself. If I allow myself to be miserable for one more day, then I have only added to my loss by giving up today."

CHAPTER SEVEN

Becoming Your Own Love Doctor

Much of the success of any therapy depends on the degree of trust between the doctor and the patient: the doctor's trust in the patient's commitment to move toward recovery as well as the patient's trust that his doctor will help him actually do this. So far in this book I have tried to help you gain a better understanding of what you feel and why you feel the way you do. Now it is time for you to call on your own capacity for self-therapy and self-healing.

The personal growth you've experienced up to this point—and will continue to experience—comes from the active part you have taken in your recovery. Think of yourself as your own therapist, your own love doctor, as you continue to move yourself through the final stages of loveshock. Ultimately, it is because you have taken control of your emotions, combined with your desire to get better and the passing of time, that you are recovering. When you take control of your emotions you have more control over your life.

In the difficult fourth stage of resignation or saying goodbye, you release the relationship from your psyche so that you can be free to begin to rebuild your life. Now, to continue that rebuilding process, you need to strengthen your courage and self-esteem.

YOUR EMOTIONAL SURVIVAL SKILLS

Throughout the book you have expanded your emotional survival skills with different exercises and therapies to get you through the early, critical stages of loveshock. These exercises and therapies are tools that you can continue to use any time you are going through a difficult emotional period, and you will want to use them whenever you feel yourself zigzagging or experiencing a loveshock flashback. (Even in the last two stages of rebuilding and resolution, you may still suffer setbacks.)

In summary, here are some of the most valuable exercises to help you through the final stages of loveshock recovery:

Self-Monitoring

As you evaluate your behavior and actions on a daily basis, self-monitoring provides you with the opportunity to step outside of yourself and watch what's going on. Self-awareness and self-knowledge enhance personal growth, especially during a loveshock experience. If you are totally honest with yourself, self-monitoring will alert you to any destructive habits or patterns that are forming—especially excessive smoking, eating, or drinking. This exercise is not intended to make you feel bad about yourself. It is intended to help you grow from your mistakes and move you through loveshock with a minimal amount of pain. Self-monitoring can be done by recording your feelings on tape, keeping a written journal, or making a simple list of the day's activities and how you felt while doing them. Or you can just take ten minutes, once or twice a day, to have an internal dialogue with yourself about what you are doing, how you feel, and how you think you are progressing. This provides you with perspective on how you are moving through your loveshock.

Thought-Blocking Technique

Every time you start thinking about your ex or feel yourself wallowing in self-pity, you instantly say to yourself, *"STOP!"* Then shift your thoughts to something equally compelling, or engross yourself in an activity that will divert your attention (see below), in spite of yourself. The more you practice this technique, the more effective it becomes.

Compelling Diverters

Any constructive activity or interest that you can focus your energy on—the very same energy that up until now you've invested in your love relationship—can be an effective diverter. Compelling diverters can be the shock absorbers of loveshock, with a bonus: at the end of loveshock you may have developed a new skill, learned a new sport, gotten a better job, or improved your appearance.

Relaxation Techniques

Develop safe, nonaddictive ways to get through high stress, panic, and anxiety periods. Some of my patients' favorites are exercising; long, hot baths with soothing music; massage; dancing; deep breathing; painting; going to the movies; playing a musical instrument; needlepoint and other crafts.

Power of Positive Suggestions

As you repeat different affirmations over and over again—such as, "My loveshock is ending, "I grow stronger every day," "I am in control"—they sink into your subconscious mind. Your subconscious will eventually begin to support the affirmation, turning your negative thoughts around. Every time you start to think, "I'm so miserable," replace it with, "I grow stronger every day."

Reminders

Affirmation notes, strategically placed, will also be very helpful. For instance, a *"STOP! DON'T CALL!"* placed by every phone will help you maintain self-control when you're tempted to pick up the phone and reconnect. Also, don't forget your list of the positive aspects of your life taped to your bathroom mirror, ready to be recited out loud as you stare at yourself and remind yourself how much you have going for you.

Let Someone Be Your 911

Create a personal support system of friends and family members who say it's okay to call them when you are tempted to call your ex or when you're just feeling down or lonely. Also, consider your church or temple or other organizations for additional emotional support.

When in Doubt, Reach Out

If you feel that you are completely out of control and you fear that you might do something self-destructive or desperate, reach out for help immediately. See a physician or have a trusted friend or physician refer you to a counselor or therapist for help. Or contact your community mental health association. Also, look to the many twelve-step self-help programs (Alcoholics Anonymous, Overeaters Anonymous, Narcotics Anonymous, etc.) that are available if you find yourself starting to escape through self-destructive means such as drugs, alcohol, or compulsive eating.

THE ROLE OF FAMILY AND FRIENDS

Your family and friends are a valuable emotional resource during loveshock. But be careful not to abuse their compassion and understanding. Make sure that it really is all right to call them at any hour, and be appreciative of the fact that they are there for you. As they have made themselves available to you, return the generosity. I remind you of this because it is not unusual during loveshock to get so wrapped up in your pesonal problems, so emotionally needy, that you forget about the importance of giving back. Treat your trusted friend or family member to a movie or dinner out. Make the effort to remove yourself from your problems by asking yourself, "Now what can I do for him or her?"

One of the hazards of loveshock is that you may become very tiresome as you discuss the same situations and events over and over again. Caught up in your pain, you may be unaware that every story you share you have already told many times before. In doing so, you may alienate and actually burn out the very people you are depending on for emotional support. They may even begin to dread your phone calls.

How do you know when enough is enough? Follow what I call the three strike principle. That is, if you've discussed the same topic or told the same story three times to the same person, either don't bring it up again or first ask whether your friend would mind discussing it with you once more. Ask for an honest answer, and don't be hurt if he or she suggests that you see a movie or go shopping together instead. And when you are out together, don't discuss your misery. It's always easier to talk about *your* pain, so make it a point to discuss your friend's concerns and interests. This will enhance your friendship and help divert, and maybe even end, your obsessional thinking.

If you need to continue discussing a particular feeling or problem, consult a counselor, therapist, or minister— someone whose job is to listen and counsel. Be aware that every friend and relative, however sympathetic, eventually grows tired of listening to your problems.

MAKING YOUR OWN LOVESHOCK TAPE

In my work as a psychotherapist I have been particularly impressed by the role of what psychologists call "the phenomenon of overlearning" in motivating and changing behavior. "Overlearning" means repeatedly hearing or otherwise being exposed to certain concepts or key phrases. When these concepts and key phrases are appropriate to the listener, they begin to influence conscious and subconscious thoughts.

This technique is used all the time by advertisers to motivate us to purchase different products. A classic example is a commercial for the American Express card: you may not remember the last time you saw the commercial, but you'll probably remember the slogan, "Don't leave home without it."

A kind of brainwashing, you can use this technique as a positive tool to ease you through your loveshock by simply making a tape that you can listen to as often as necessary.

I have all of my loveshock patients make a tape about the dynamics of the relationship that has ended: what was good about it, when and why it had to change, why it had to end, and in what ways it is beneficial that it has ended. Such a tape can help you understand the difference between what once was and what now is. If this relationship was self-destructive for you and you feel that you are moth-to-flaming, make sure that you listen frequently to the tape to remind yourself of all the reasons that this relationship was bad for you. When you find yourself getting bored, make a new tape with a variation of the same theme.

Whenever you are tempted to call your ex or do anything that will draw you back into the relationship, listen to the tape. Listen to it when you are filled with self-doubt. Slip it into your Walkman and listen to it while you are exercising. Auditory stimuli are extremely powerful. And hearing *your own voice* telling you the truth over and over again will create a greater impact, making it easier for you to maintain self-control.

We all have a "psyche tape" playing in our mind, composed of bits and pieces of all of our experiences up to the present time. Often the reason you get stuck in one of the stages of loveshock is that your psyche tape is playing a fantasy that you want to believe: "X still loves me. I'm still in love with X. The relationship will be reconciled and we will continue our life together . . ."

If you find that this sort of fantasy tape is playing in your psyche, constantly programming you with a message that is not productive, you should make yourself a truth tape to pitch the correct message. Begin by saying, "It's over. This is why it ended . . ."

I can't stress enough how valuable the loveshock tapes can be. I've had hundreds of loveshock patients make their own loveshock tapes, and all have felt that making the tape and constantly listening to it helped them at least maintain self-control when they were tempted to do something that ultimately might have caused them more pain. Others have reported that their tapes gave them a more profound sense of what happened and why their relationships ended, as hidden messages surfaced in the tapes after they had listened to them several times. Perhaps they were only reinterpreting their original statements; whatever the case, the tapes seem to be very beneficial.

ANXIETY CONTROL TECHNIQUES

Anxiety attacks can be frequent and quite severe during loveshock. They can take different forms and can trigger different compulsive behaviors. You may feel so unnerved that you would rather escape through excess than suffer another moment of anxiety. Suddenly you find yourself drinking excessively, taking drugs, eating compulsively, or maybe even gambling—anything to divert you from the anxiety that comes from your loneliness and your hurt.

I have two different relaxation techniques that you can use to manage anxiety attacks. The first one is a modification of one of the most powerful methods of relaxation that I know of; it is called the Jacobson Relaxation Technique. (Dr. Jacobson was a world-reknowned cardiologist who developed this technique to assist his cardiac patients and others to cope with severe stress.)

Take the phone off the hook so that you are not disturbed. Sit in a comfortable chair or lie on your bed. Close your eyes. Begin to listen to the gentle melody of your breathing—in and out. Now each time you breathe out, repeat to yourself, "Calm and relax."

After a minute or two of unwinding this way, keeping your eyes closed, take the deepest breath you can and hold it for around thirty seconds. When it begins to hurt, let go.

Take a second very deep breath. As you do so and hold it, feel all the pain, any loneliness or depression, any anger toward yourself or the other person. Really feel it and live it for that moment. And when you are ready, let it all go with a big deep breath.

Now focus on breathing slowly and deeply for a few moments, before you begin the second part of this exercise. In the second part you will make all of your muscles tense and firm. By tensing your muscles, you are actually forcing any accumulated tension to be released. When you tense your muscles and then suddenly release them, they react by actually relaxing and releasing the tension.

Continue breathing slowly and deeply, with your eyes closed, and gently begin to tense your muscles. Begin with your feet and work your way up your body. Tense your calves, your thighs, your abdomen, your chest, your neck, your face, the muscles around your eyes, your arms, your hands. And clench your fists. When your whole body is tense, think of it as one piece of wood. Hold the tension until it starts to hurt. If you feel any emotional pain, any depression, any sadness, or any anger—this is the time to let it go.

As you feel all of these emotions leaving your body, imagine your legs going limp, just like two pieces of rope. Feel the muscles in your abdomen and chest going limp like rope too. Feel your arms and hands going limp. Now feel the muscles of your jaw relaxing so that your teeth don't even touch. Feel the muscles around your eyes relaxing so that your eyelids seem heavy on your eyes. Breathe slowly and breathe deeply.

With every easy, deep breath you take, feel yourself becoming more relaxed. It feels so good to relax. And now, breathing slowly and deeply, see yourself happy and smiling. You are laughing again. You are at peace.

During this exercise you may feel as if your body is floating. Or you may feel that your body is melting into the bed or the chair. You are feeling calm and relaxed, as you listen to the gentle melody of your breathing.

Stay in this relaxed state for about five minutes. Think of it as your mini-vacation in the midst of a stressful day. Then, as you prepare to bring yourself out of it, see yourself resting on a beautiful beach—serene and in control of your life. As you continue to feel calm and relaxed, acknowledge that it's okay to worry at times and maybe even to be a little anxious. Now see yourself happy, managing, and taking control of your life.

And as you are feeling totally in control, slowly count from one to three. When you reach three, affirm to yourself, "I am in control of my life. After all that I've been through, I'm not going to let anxiety take over my life." Continue to breathe deeply and slowly as you bring yourself out of this state of deep relaxation.

You will be amazed at how refreshed you feel afterwards. This is the perfect way to release anxiety while you are at home. You may want to follow this technique with a warm bath.

If you are having an anxiety attack in a public place, you can release it with this simple technique that takes about sixty seconds: while sitting in a chair, first calm yourself with some deep breathing, slowly inhaling and exhaling. Now begin to tense all of the muscles in your body. Begin with your feet, as you did in the first technique, and work your way up your body. (You don't have to close your eyes or clench the muscles of your face if people are around.)

Once your whole body is tense and tight like a piece of wood, bring together your thumb and index finger so that they form an O. Clench the two of them together as hard as you can. You can do this with just one hand or with both hands.

As you clench, feel all the anxiety being drained into these two (or four) fingers. Repeat to yourself, "Drain, drain." When you are ready, let these fingers go. As they separate, imagine yourself flicking away all of that anxiety. Repeat this technique three or four times.

Also remember that one of the best ways to release stress, tension, and anxiety is through exercise. I often recommend more exercise therapy than psychotherapy for loveshock patients; sometimes this is the first time they have actively exercised in years. Besides all the gyms and health clubs available, there are numerous exercise videos that you can use at home. Invest in a stationary bike and some weights. Many people feel more comfortable exercising at home if they are out of shape; there is no need to add the additional anxiety of "How do I look?" What's important is that you find a means of exercise that you will do regularly. Exercise increases neurochemicals, called endorphins, which biochemically help to reduce anxiety. They are a natural mood elevator.

Not only will you feel better in general and have less anxiety when you exercise regularly—you'll start to look better too. Loveshock often makes you look pale and drawn; the emotional pain radiates from your face. Exercising will make you appear more serene because you are more serene after you exercise.

LEARNING FROM YOUR PERSONAL HISTORY: THE CAPITAL GAINS OF LOVE

When you make your personal statement as you travel through resignation, clearly confronting what went wrong in the relationship and why it ended, and taking responsibility for your role in the breakup, *you don't have to lose your personal history*. While you are releasing the last of the love relationship from your psyche, you should also try to preserve what was positive in the relationship and weave it into your new life. This is what I call the *capital gains of love*. Perhaps you had children, perhaps you traveled a lot or learned a new skill or expanded in your career while you were in the relationship. Any of these things can be very valuable in your future, because they contribute to who you are as a person.

But often it is difficult to figure out exactly how to integrate your past into the present and future. More than one loveshock patient has asked me, "When it's all over, where do you put the memories?"

One of the problems of loveshock is that while you are trying to release yourself from the past, you tend to negate everything—including any positive experiences that you gained by being in the relationship. This was Les's problem. He felt that the only thing that he got out of his seven-year relationship with Sherry was a lot of humiliation when she left him for a younger man. Consequently, he thought that he had nothing to show for all of the time and energy he had put into their relationship. However, it only took one question from me to make him aware of something he had gotten out of the relationship, something that would come in handy in future relationships.

"Les, I want you to look at your whole relationship and tell me what you think the best part of it was. There had to be something that kept you together for seven years. What were the pleasurable moments in the relationship?"

He sat quietly for a few minutes and then suddenly perked up. "The sex was fabulous. Sherry was absolutely incredible in bed: in fact, we did things together that I thought you could only think about. On a daily basis she was moody and difficult to live with, but once you got her in bed she really turned on."

Regardless of all else, Les had developed sexual expertise during his seven years with Sherry because she had been a very willing partner. And although she had left him to be with a younger man, he knew that he was a good lover. This was one insecurity that he wouldn't have to deal with when he was ready to get involved again. In fact, he had gained a skill that would serve him well. "Even on that last horrible day, two hours before she moved out, we made exquisite love on the living-room floor. While I'm still not sure why she feels so drawn to this other guy, I do know that I more than satisifed her sexual appetite."

Occasionally I get a patient who has been emotionally battered to the point of mental cruelty. This is someone who justifiably feels that there is nothing to be salvaged from the relationship, except perhaps the knowledge of what he or she doesn't want in the next relationship (if there is to be one). Sometimes, the experience has been so horrible that afterwards the patient becomes love phobic—afraid to love at all. It may take additional therapy for the patient to overcome the love phobia, to be willing to take a chance on love.

This was true for Janis, an executive secretary who had given up her career to stay home and look after Brent's needs when she was twenty-seven. Brent was a charming Englishman who had entered the import-export firm where she worked and swept her off her feet. "God, he was so good-looking, with those steel blue eyes and black, wavy hair. I should have known he'd end up being trouble. I resisted at first, but he wore me down with the flowers, poems, and romantic dinners. I didn't think men like this really existed, except in romance novels."

Three months after they met they were living to-gether. Brent maintained the charm, passion, and in-tensity for several months, and finally Janis agreed to marry him.

"After almost a year of wonderful, old-fashioned courtship, even after we were living together, I was convinced that I had finally found the perfect man for me. I even agreed to give up everything I had worked so hard to gain, because he said he wanted a real wife—not some career woman. Well, two months after I said, 'I do,' I wished that I had said, 'I don't.' Suddenly, he started coming home late, often drunk, and then would demand his dinner after I had put everything away. He would complain that the apartment wasn't clean enough or that the laundry wasn't done right. He began to belittle me and make me feel as if I were nothing. And one of the worst things that he did was put me down in front of our friends. I really started feeling like I was living in another century, when women were treated like slaves."

Janis looked away for a moment before she could continue. "When I miscarried, he never even came to the hospital. My girlfriend brought me home. And for days he wouldn't speak to me. It was as though I had committed some horrible sin . . . After five years of this, I think that I've finally had it. I mean, I'm only thirty-two, but I feel all used up. What were the good times? I don't remember anymore. Whatever they were, they got buried in the insanity of this relationship."

While I tried to reassure Janis that there was some good that had come out of all this in terms of self-knowledge, her knowledge of her own needs, all she could say was "What a fool I've been!"

Finally, I looked at her and said, "That's a very healthy statement. It shows that you are in touch with the reality of the situation. While what you are telling me is very negative, you are at the same time saying that you have learned from it." Janis would have been in trouble if she were thinking about going back into the relationship or idealizing it even though she had been so mentally abused.

"What amazes me more than anything, Dr. Gullo, was how he deceived me. I mean, we were together for almost a year and even lived together before I agreed to marry him. What could I have done differently?"

"Probably nothing. Unfortunately, we can't run a relationship check, like a credit check, on people before we agree to marry them. And there are some people that change in personality once they get what they want. Not until then do you see their real nature. You're not the first person this has happened to. Perhaps the only mistake you made was to give up your career and then center your life completely around his. We all need to maintain our own identities. You probably should have insisted on keeping your job, at least part-time, and to some degree maintained your independence. Brent is a taker. And the more you gave, the more he took. Now you know that this is not the type of person who will ever make you happy."

"But his change was so radical. How do I know who to trust?"

"Unfortunately, Janis, there are no guarantees; that's why it takes courage to love. Sometimes you can only operate by instinct. However, again I stress that your first concern when you get involved with anyone is for you to maintain your own identity—this means your career, your friends, and any interests you had before you met this person. While you may have to make some compromises, it is unwise to give your whole life over to another person."

I encouraged Janis to think of this relationship as a kind of dress rehearsal for the next one. While she had suffered terribly, she was now very aware of what her personal needs were and realized that she had the strength to endure. Perhaps she had gained some insights that would help her to have better future relationships. In this case, although it had caused her a tremendous amount of pain, what she had learned was her capital gain of love.

This was Janis's first loveshock experience. I reassured her that if or when she ever went through loveshock again, it would not be as paintful.

"Well, that's a relief, Dr. Gullo, but why is the first loveshock experience often the most painful?"

"Because people who go through all the stages of loveshock always grow stronger as a result of it. Think of it as a strengthening of the emotional immune system. And after it's finally over, they realize, often amazed, that they have survived and grown stronger. When loveshock comes again, they've developed coping skills that they can utilize again. And because they know what to expect, what's happening to them is not so frightening. They also find it easier to be in control of their emotions, because they know their loveshock will end."

It was important to help Janis focus on what positive things had happened to her since the breakup. I reminded her that, in her case, just ending the relationship was positive.

"I find that I've cut back on my smoking, because I'm not so nervous anymore. My girlfriend is letting me share her apartment until I can find a new job. The lawyers are still arguing over a settlement, so money is tight. Also, I've stopped drinking. You know I never really drank at all until I met Brent, and then suddenly I was having wine every night. He was a real connoisseur and believed a meal incomplete without a couple of bottles of wine. It's strange; now that I'm alone again I seem more like my old self."

It actually wasn't strange at all. Many people are like chameleons—especially when they are in love. As their insecurities begin to surface, often they will alter their behavior to please the other person. In the process, they begin gradually to lose their own identity as they are, in a sense, absorbed by the other person. Ending the relationship, even as the rejectee, is essential to the recovery of their self-identity.

PROMOTING YOUR OWN PSYCHOLOGICAL GROWTH

Quite often the loveshock experience makes apparent a much larger issue: your need to promote your own psychological growth. Again, I remind you how important it is that you release yourself from the burden of being perfect. It's okay to make a mistake and make a fool of yourself. In fact, as I pointed out to Janis, to acknowledge that you've made a mistake is a sign of psychological growth. In accepting our humanity we must accept our imperfections; they're a part of life.

Accepting the end of a relationship and acknowledging it to have been a mistake is a growth step—although a painful one. That's why it's extremely important that you build up your self-esteem by involving yourself in positive activities and in positive relationships.

If, like Janis, you let your spouse become your whole life, you have realized that you can never rely on just one person to be your sole source of emotional support.

That's unrealistic, and it's too much of a burden to place on anyone.

Apply the same principle to your emotions that you do to your finances—diversify! Not only does a range of interests promote your psychological growth, but it makes your life full, and it makes you very interesting to other people. Now is your chance to become a part of the office group—people you may barely know socially because you always had to rush right home to be with your spouse. Join everyone after work for drinks, softball, or the bowling team. Become active with your church, community service group, or arts council. Get involved with a cause that you believe in. Become a part of the mainstream of life. This way, when you lose some part of your life or someone in your life, you won't be so devastated: these emotional shock absorbers will cushion the blow.

Also, take the time to spoil yourself regularly. Whether it's having a massage, exercising, having a manicure, or just a long bath—indulge. They may seem like little things, but they reinforce your sense of self-love, which may have been inadequate even before your loveshock began.

The more you help yourself, the better you become. As your self-confidnce grows, an inner contentment grows with it. Suddenly the future does not seem so hopeless, for you are reaching out to take an active part in life again.

CHAPTER EIGHT

How to Know When You Are Ready to Love Again

You wake up one morning, make your coffee, and sit down to read the paper. You feel satisfied and happy, just by yourself, as you get ready to begin your day. Business has been going well and perhaps you're up for a promotion. A long workweek is ahead of you, but it doesn't matter because you have a special ski weekend to look forward to. There's a promise dancing on the horizon, the promise of new friendships and maybe even a little romance.

Suddenly you realize that the pain is gone. Your first thoughts no longer focus on what your ex is doing; in fact, you really couldn't care one way or the other because you are too busy rebuilding your life. The bad memories of the breakup are fading away. You may still suffer from an occasional loveshock flashback, which quickly passes. But there is no doubt: your life is no longer centered on your love loss, and your energy is no longer focused on recovering from it. You have traveled beyond your personal pain and have overcome many of the problems that were a part of it. Maybe, for you, it was obsessional thinking, rebounding, and numerous fears that once overwhelmed your daily existence. Now you are very self-aware and self-protective, determined not to repeat any of your previous mistakes.

In the stage of rebuilding, you now feel as if your life is finally yours—that you are able to manage it and that you have your emotions back under control. And perhaps to your surprise, you find yourself wanting love to be a part of your life again.

Rather than avoiding socializing or just throwing yourself into your work, you're putting yourself in situations where you may have the opportunity to meet someone new. Or maybe you're encouraging your friends to set up blind dates or dinner partners for you. Ironically, the very same people whom you resented five or six months ago for trying to fix you up you now encourage.

However, as much as you desire to get on with your life, you may feel a certain apprehension about dating again. This is perfectly normal when you are coming out of loveshock, it is to be expected if you have ended a long- term relationship: your last date may have been twenty years ago. That's why most of my loveshock patients have found that easing back into life as a single is best done through transitional relationships.

MAKING TRANSITIONAL RELATIONSHIPS
   WORK FOR YOU

Whether it is sharing a movie, dinner out, a lot of telephone talk, or even a safe sexual encounter, don't underestimate the value of short-term relationships, or what I call *transitional relationships*. They can be especially valuable in helping you reconnect with your intimate feelings in a relaxed and nonthreatening environment without demands or pressures. Think of transitional relationships as a way to test the water, as a way to help you better understand your personal needs. And after all the emotional pain you have suffered during loveshock, transitional relationships can even make you feel lovable and desirable again as they fuel your self-esteem.

It's not unusual for a transitional relationship to go beyond a couple of dates and turn into a wonderful friendship, in which you can share some of life's burdens and some of life's joys. This was true for Bill and Joyce. I had counseled Bill during the darkest days of his loveshock and encouraged him to try transitional relationships when he felt that he was ready.

When Bill asked Joyce out, he knew that she was not the next woman he would marry. But she was nice. And she made him laugh and made him feel good about himself. Having been through so much emotional pain, he found it to be a tremendous relief to go out with a woman and just have a good time. They would hug and exchange quick kisses on the cheek—but that was it, and that was fine for both of them.

Eventually Joyce also started dating Sidney and they became romantically involved. But she and Bill still remained close friends and continued to look out for one another's well-being. When Bill got pneumonia, Joyce was there with the chicken soup before she spent the evening with Sidney. And when her car broke down, Bill gave Joyce rides to and from work until it was repaired.

When Joyce and Sidney married, Bill was thrilled for

his good friend—but sad because they would be moving to another state. "No matter where Joyce is, I'll always love her as my friend and be eternally grateful to her for making me feel like a part of the human race again. What started out as a transitional relationship was responsible for restoring a lot of my self-confidence— besides turning into a wonderful friendship."

In a transitional relationship you have nothing to lose and everything to gain because there are no promises, obligations, or strings attached. You only have to give what you want to give and you can take as much as you want of what the other person is offering. This may be the first chance you have had in years to be totally honest in a relationship.

However, keep in mind that in a transitional relationship you are still vulnerable to rejection, even though this is not a serious relationship. You may date someone a few times and wish to continue, while the other person may not want to go out with you again. There is no reason to take this rejection seriously or to allow it to lower your self-esteem. Or you may experience a partial rejection, as you desire more from the transitional relationship than the other person is prepared to give.

When Steve and Diane began dating, both were coming out of loveshock experiences and focusing on rebuilding their lives. Steve hated eating alone, so he and Diane became frequent dining partners. One night, after a lot of wine, Diane began to snuggle up to Steve, suggesting that they spend the rest of their evening together in bed. Steve hated sexual pressure, partially because his relationship with his ex-wife had been so performance-oriented.

"Suddenly, as I was about to say yes, I realized that

I didn't have to have sex with Diane if I didn't want to. This was something that I just wasn't ready for. What a relief to know that I could say no, that I didn't have to pretend, because my relationship with Diane was transitional. At that moment my attitude was that if my saying no meant that I would never see her again, so be it. Realizing this gave me the most wonderful sense of freedom and ease! Fortunately, Diane didn't push it and we continued seeing one another. Two months later I found myself ready for sex, and Diane and I began the sexual dimension of our relationship. But we always had the understanding, that there were no strings attached. Right now we're close, but we also date other people. It's the only way because neither one of us is ready to take the next step."

Often, if all you have known is a long-term relationship, you may see a relationship as an all-or-nothing proposition. In other words, if it is not going to lead to marriage, then what is the point? Why waste the time? If this is your point of view, you are losing sight of the fact that all relationships provide you with the opportunity to enhance social skills, and maybe even love skills, that may have diminished during the course of your past relationship.

You should consider transitional relationships to be opportunities to learn about yourself as well as about the different types of people that exist. Think of them as your chance to grow emotionally as you meet new people, to get in touch with your specific needs, and to learn what is involved in a relationship before you commit yourself to one again.

INTIMATE AGAIN

After loveshock, being intimate again is never easy. For men, regardless of their age, there is often a period of impotency during and after their loveshock. And almost every woman I've counseled has reported going through a period of fleeing from any sexuality. As Emily, twenty-eight and very attractive told me, "It took me two months of dating before I'd let a guy kiss me good night. I even found a handshake awkward!"

Both lack of sexual ability and lack of interest are normal parts of the aftershock of loveshock. Often I'll hear from my patients, "Now on top of everything else I've been through, I've got to deal with this?"

As thirty-one-year-old Walt so vividly told me, "Here I was with this beautiful woman in my arms, and God, you know I was really scared because I couldn't get it up. But the scariest part of all was that I didn't have any desire to! I was totally deflated in all areas! It destroyed what little self-confidence I had, because all I could think of was what this woman must think of me. It was so embarrassing for both of us!"

To be intimate again is to expose yourself completely. It's not just taking off your clothes, but stripping yourself to the vulnerability that comes with sexuality. This is why it is so important that you don't push yourself to be intimate until you are really sure that you are ready. Steve had the right idea when he said no to Diane: otherwise he could have ended up in the same predicament that Walt did. And since sexuality had been an issue in his marriage, it would only have added to his anxiety.

Usually I advise my patients just to take it slow and let time in cooperation with the natural flow of their hormones be their therapist. However, if you find that you are obsessing on your lack of interest or sexual inability, seek professional help. Focusing too much on the problem, worrying that you'll never want to or be able to have sex again, could just make it worse.

Being intimate with someone new is usually more difficult for older people who are coming out of a twenty- or thirty-year marriage. For them even the idea of a simple date may be terrifying because it is so unfamiliar. They may also experience what I call a conflict of generations: confusion about how to act on a date because dating values and guidelines have changed so drastically over the years.

If this is your situation, you may feel frightened or even panicked the first time a person calls to ask you out. This is a normal reaction, and if you have any interest at all, try to say yes. You have to begin somewhere. The first few dates you have may be awkward because you are simply out of practice, so if they don't go well and you're uncomfortable, don't be hard on yourself. Accept these feelings as another part of your growth process—and don't give up!

Beatrice married Arthur when she was eighteen, had four children with him, and woke up one day at the age of fifty-four to an empty bed and a note. In the note he told her that his leaving had nothing to do with her— that he was confused about the meaning of his life, felt lost in the corporate world, and knew that it was time that he searched for the truth, whatever it was. At first Beatrice thought, "He'll get this out of his system and he'll be back."

A month later she was served with divorce papers and offered a more-than-fair settlement that amazed even her lawyer. Beatrice was in grief and a state of confusion for months as she tried to understand what had actually happened. It took her two years before she could even think about the possibility of dating because she always thought that Arthur would come back.

The first date she had ended after an hour and a half. She got nauseated and had to go home. "Not only was I afraid, Dr. Gullo, sitting next to someone I barely knew in a dark movie theater, but I felt as if I were betraying Arthur. I felt so guilty, being out with another man. And I feel so inadequate."

"In what way?"

"With my appearance. I mean, what if I did meet someone, and we really liked one another, and it led to sex? The only man who has seen me without clothes, besides Arthur, is my doctor."

Beatrice was voicing the fear and concern of many older people, most frequently women, whose bodies are no longer one of their primary assets. And any guilt or betrayal they feel is natural because they were in their previous relationship for such a long time. For many, the only person that they have ever had sex with is their ex. Unfortunately, the guilt feelings only fuel their negative self-image, making it all the more difficult for them to take those intitial steps as a single person.

I advised Beatrice to take it slow and to do what she could to make herself feel better about her appearance. Four months later, Beatrice had joined an exercise class to tone her body and had purchased a more chic, contemporary wardrobe. When we last talked, she was dating two different men regularly—but keeping them at arm's length.

Joan has just turned fifty and has been divorced for three years. She is quite wealthy and travels in a glittering social circle. Her hallmark is her extensive art collection: it became her compelling diverter during her loveshock. Two months ago she met a younger man, ten years to be exact, who keeps inviting her away for weekends. He's a very successful graphics designer and is crazy about her. They go to the ballet and the opera together. He escorts her to social events. In many ways they're perfect for one another—but she keeps making up excuses about why she can't go away with him for the weekend, because if she does go, she knows that they will probably end up in bed together. And she is convinced that once he sees her without clothes, she'll never see him again.

I've suggested to her that she go on a diet, hire a personal trainer (someone who will come to her home regularly and help her exercise), and even look into plastic surgery. If it's that important to her, and the only thing that's keeping her from realizing what could become her next love relationship, she should take action. Money is not an issue for her. In fact, she's lucky because she is one of the privileged who can afford to totally redesign herself, if she wants to.

But she resists. And things remain the same, as she and Vince play their cat-and-mouse game of "Will you go away with me?" She reasons that, as uncomfortable as the issue of intimacy makes her feel because of her body, she is content just the way she is. Joan is not psychologically ready for physical intimacy.

Whether it's from lack of sexual desire, the inability to perform, or being uncomfortable with their nudity, for men like Walt and Steve, and women like Emily, Beatrice, and Joan, intimacy brings with it a lot of psychological confusion. Sometimes the confusion is one of the last lingering reactions to your loveshock: you are afraid that any intimacy will ultimately lead to your getting hurt again. And for many, it is a terrible shock to go from having a complete sexual relationship with just one person all of your adult life to suddenly having to decide something as basic as "Do I kiss her (or him) or "Do I allow him (or her) to kiss me—and if I do, where will it lead?"

If you are having a difficult time reintegrating intimacy into your life, I recommend practicing what I call *phased intimacy*. That means making physical contact with another person *very slowly,* step by step. Until you feel comfortable with the step you've taken, you go no further. For instance, you may begin simply by holding hands. Not until you feel completely at ease with this would you progress to hugging and then kissing. And then you would ease into long embraces.

I think of phased intimacy as a kind of necessary sexual rehabilitation after a very painful emotional breakup. I compare it to the physical rehabilitation that is often necessary after you break an arm or leg. The limb must be strengthened before it can completely function again. The same is true in intimacy. You must be emotionally strong and comfortable with your sexuality before you can completely function again.

You should communicate to the other person exactly how you feel and how important it is that he or she lets you go slowly. Don't allow yourself to be talked into something that you are not ready for. If the time isn't right, don't be afraid to say no. Again, this is where transitional relationships are invaluable. If another person places demands on you that you feel you are not ready to fulfill, there is no reason that you have to continue the relationship. As one patient told me, "After having survived loveshock with my sanity intact, the last thing I'm going to tolerate is someone coming on to me, still persisting after I say no, before I'm ready."

While you may feel that you are ready to love again, seeking out new people and new relationships, allow yourself the time you need before you become intimate. Don't feel that you have to rush it. When you are really ready to physically reach out and touch, you will experience, in your comfort and ease, the beauty of truly connecting with another person once again.

CHAPTER NINE

Loving Again

Traveling through loveshock is a journey that you are unlikely ever to forget, nor should you, because what you have learned can prove invaluable in helping you to create your present and future happiness. While it may not be completely obvious yet, you have grown from the pain of your loveshock and are wiser for it. Loveshock forced you to confront yourself and different aspects of your life, as your personal flaws, your pitfalls, and your anxieties appeared. For many of you this was the first time in your life that you evaluated and dealt with your emotions so openly and honestly. Ultimately, your personal truth emerged as you became acutely aware of your needs. And as your fears and frustrations unfolded, you developed greater self-awareness.

After all that you have been through, having reached the final stage of resolution, you now know what gives you joy in a relationship, what situations you can tolerate and can compromise on, and what you find unbearable. Values and ideals that may have been dormant for many years have reemerged and become an important part of your life, along with any additional beliefs that have developed. And with all that you have learned and gained from your personal pain, not only are you able to love again, but you stand a better chance of developing a more satisfying love relationship because you have been through so much and you know yourself so well. You also realize that simply to love is not enough to sustain a love relationship.

PUTTING THE PAST INTO PERSPECTIVE

Before you can love again, completely and unimpaired, you must put your past pain into proper perspective. This means releasing any destructive feelings of anger or bitterness that can still linger even in the final stage of resolution. You may experience an occasional zigzag back to setting blame, set off by a loveshock flashback, that stirs up old feelings. Or perhaps you feel angry and bitter toward love in general, because you've been hurt. And you may even find yourself turning your anger inward, against yourself, which many psychotherapists believe to be the basis for depression.

While you may have a right to your anger, don't let it become the focus of your life—for your own sake, and for the sake of those around you. Life is too short for you to spend your time and thoughts consumed with rage. In the end it is just another form, and a destructive one at that, of hanging on to the past. Work on releasing yourself from the negative aspects of this rage. If you don't, you are likely to displace it onto others, especially your family, children, and friends—or even a new lover. Ultimately, all your relationships will begin to suffer, for you will be repelling love. Remember that no one is more unlovable or unattractive, regardless of physical appearance, than an angry, bitter person.

Philosopher Albert Schweitzer observed that "the tragedy of life is what dies inside a man while he lives." Don't let your loveshock experience make you afraid or unable to love again. For if you permit the failed reltionship and your loveshock experience to make you afraid to love again, you will have lost more than the person and the relationship; you will have lost one of the most central of all human qualities—the ability to love, which is the essence of our humanity.

To continue to live happily in the face of the unhappiness you have endured in your life requires that you develop the capacity to distance yourself from the emotional pain of the past. This is an important part of your psychological growth. As I have frequently observed—and as you will have realized while traveling through loveshock—time and your psyche should move you away from this pain. However, it may take extra effort on your part to release its final vestiges. Remember that one of the joys of being in resolution is that it is your opportunity to make a fresh start, without the burdens of the past but with the added advantage of having grown from your personal pain.

If you find that you still obsess on anger or bitterness, employ the thought-blocking technique whenever these negative feelings surface. Again, this means telling yourself, "STOP!" and moving yourself away from these negative feelings as you engross yourself in one of your compelling diverters. Also, remind yourself of how much emotionally you have overcome and continue to focus on the new life cycle you are beginning in resolution.

Remember Beatrice, who woke up one morning to

an empty bed and a note from Arthur? One of the reasons it took her two years to even think about dating was that she had so much bitterness within her. But she realized that her bitterness would not change her situation. So every time it popped up while she was at home, she would go out and weed her garden. "With every weed that I pull comes a *'STOP!'* I don't stop weeding until my anger is gone; sometimes I end up weeding a whole flower bed! Sometimes I'll pick a beautiful bouquet afterwards and take it over to the hospital where I do volunteer work. It redirects my energy from the anger I feel to caring about the needs of others."

While you are releasing the last of these negative feelings, guard against discussing your past relationship in a derogatory way. It's unwise to bring into a potential new relationship bitter comments or remarks because you may be misunderstood. Only you know what you've suffered as you have gone through *your* loveshock, and discussing your past in this way only clouds what could and should be a clean slate. When questions do come up about your previous relationship, try to speak about it objectively and mention some of the good things that came out of it. However, if you presently feel incapable of doing this or uncomfortable in discussing it at all, say so and change the subject. This protects your privacy and keeps you from saying something that you may later regret. It also prevents you from dwelling on the pain of the past as you continue to move forward.

A positive way to utilize your anger is to analyze it and let it teach you something about your own emotional needs. For example, if your anger stems from betrayal, then know that loyalty is important for your happiness in your next relationship. Look for a person who embodies this quality, as well as the other essentials you value, to be your partner in developing and sustaining a meaningful relationship.

ATTRACTING THE BEST RELATIONSHIP
   FOR YOU

A leading divorce attorney once advised one of my loveshock patients that while he couldn't tell her what would guarantee her happiness in future relationships, he could tell her what would make for unhappiness in a relationship: marrying outside of her philosophy of life. His concept is brilliant because it applies to everyone and has proven true time and again. I call it *the shared philosophy of life*. I have used this concept when counseling my loveshock patients who desire to attract stable, lasting relationships into their lives.

As an example, if your idea of a satisfying relationship includes quiet evenings at home while your potential partner likes parties and traveling, you do not have a shared philosophy of life. While the two of you may be extremely attracted to one another initially and even marry, chances are that after that initial bloom of romance fades, your different life philosophies will begin to conflict. Unless a lot of concessions and compromises are made and your love is strong enough to overcome the differences, the relationship does not have a very good chance of lasting.

One of the positive aspects of the loveshock experience is that you do emerge from it with a much keener awareness of your philosophy of life. So consider your philosophy when you look at the direction a potential relationship may take; ask yourself, "If I love this person, can this person love me, in return, *in the way that*

I need to be loved?" I think that answering yes to this question is vital before seriously entering into a new relationship.

Having a shared philosophy of life doesn't mean you can't have different likes and dislikes. In fact one of the realizations that occur during loveshock is that it's important to maintain your individuality in a relationship. Many of you travelers through loveshock have only recently regained it. The essence of a shared philosophy of life is not that you're identical in outlook but that your relationship fundamentals and goals are basically the same; a shared philosophy means that most of your needs will be fulfilled just as you will be able to fulfill most of the needs of your partner. While there is no perfect relationship, a happy and satisfying one is certainly possible when your lifestyles harmoniously merge.

Most people, having gone through loveshock, prefer to avoid relationships that portend conflict—even if it means giving up some excitement as well. You may find yourself ending a relationship before it becomes serious, as you become aware of too many lifestyle differences. As Walt told me, when he began having transitional relationships, "I meet plenty of women that I could spend the night with—but never a lifetime. That takes someone special who not only understands my needs and shares my interests, but is also willing to meet me at least half way when she doesn't."

I make the general assumption that most people marry because they are in love; most marriages end, I believe, because the couple lack a shared philosophy of life and cannot meet each other's needs. While finding a partner with a shared philosophy of life does not guarantee happiness, it is certainly a positive start for a new relationship.

YOU CAN'T MARRY THE PROMISE

While many of my loveshock patients have learned this lesson from the direction their past relationship took, I still like to remind them that "they can't marry the promise." Or to be more blunt, when you involve yourself in a new relationship, remember that what you see is what you get.

Ideally we all continue to develop, improve, and grow in our relationships as well as in our professional lives. However, when you decide to commit to another relationship, realize that while the other person may have the best of intentions, *what he or she is at this very moment is the only guarantee you have.* Don't commit to a relationship because you are enticed by what he or she promises it will be. Or with the hope that you can change this person into what you think he or she should be. Approaching a new commitment this way is unfair to the other person and will only cause you tremendous frustration as he or she resists and perhaps even rebels against your attempts to play Pygmalion.

Before you make a commitment, wipe the stars out of your eyes and ask yourself these questions: "If he (or she) never becomes anything greater than what he (or she) is at the moment, is it acceptable? Can I love this person exactly as he (or she) is, including any bad habits— which may never change?" If you are unable to answer these questions with a strong yes, take time to evaluate the relationship before you proceed. This is your chance to make a clean break, with a minimal amount of pain to yourself or the other person. And realize that if there is pain now, in the initial phase of your relationship, you may experience much more pain in the future if you delay ending it. Sometimes deciding not to take action is, psychologically, the most costly decision of all.

When Matt met Vicki, he knew that she drank too much. But he idealized the relationship and really believed that he could change her. He thought that their love would cure all. Ultimately he ended up being the unwilling rejector, going in and out of the relationship until he realized that—because he was powerless over Vicki's alcoholism and could not live with her behavior—he had to end the relationship. He suffered terribly in putting an end to a relationship that should never have progressed to marriage.

WORKING TOWARD LOVE SYNERGY, OR HEALTHY LOVE

Many psychologists describe three basic types of love relationship that we can involve ourselves in: parasitic, symbiotic, and synergistic.

In a parasitic relationship, one person takes far more than he or she gives to the relationship. He or she feeds off the other person financially, emotionally, or both. Often this relationship ends when the parasite has taken all that he or she needs. A parasitic relationship can also end because the person who has done all the giving has nothing left—he or she is all used up—except what it takes to leave the relationship.

This is why Janis left Brent. She had done all the giving, while he had done all the taking. And when Janis finally left, she left out of fear—fear that somehow Brent would ultimately consume all of her.

However, Janis's role as the parasite's host, or giver, cannot be disregarded. Janis had never had a serious love relationship and was anxious to meet someone to share her life with. She had grown tired of the singles lifestyle and, as she approached her late twenties, became concerned that she was losing her physical appeal. When Brent appeared, although she resisted at first, she eventually succumbed to his charm because she was eager to have a permanent relationship. And once she was hooked she began her pattern of excessive giving because she was afraid that he would look elsewhere if she didn't; all of her girlfriends envied her, wishing that they could find a man like him.

Often a person is so desperate to be loved that he or she will give anything, including everything that he or she has, to hold on to the other person. Neither partner in this relationship is loving in a healthy, balanced way. Both are acting out of desperation and both need counseling or professional help to change the all-consuming dynamics of their relationship.

When a relationship is symbiotic, both partners feed one another. Alone they feel incomplete, as neither one of them is secure enough in his or her own identity. And even if they are miserable when they are together, as is frequently true, they are still happier together than they are apart. Sometimes this relationship is filled with mistrust and paranoia—one person becoming obsessed with what the other is doing when they are apart, even when the separation is necessary because of life's daily responsibilities.

Often the mutually possessive nature of this relationship allows for little growth within it. For many people this type of relationship works because they have limited expectations, not only of themselves but of love relationships in general. They are satisifed with what they have. Essentially, the dynamic of this relationship is "I

love you because I need you," not, "I need you because
I love you." Symbiotic relationships are very common
and often endure until death—unless one of the partners
feels the need to establish a stronger sense of self.

Joan, who is in resolution and still working toward
intimacy with Vince, the young graphics designer, left
her husband because their symbiotic relationship was
starting to smother her. "We were both so insecure,
constantly phoning one another and checking up on each
other. But when we were together, we fought and dis-
agreed over the stupidest things. One day I just realized
that while I was terrified to be on my own, I had to
leave the marriage and find out who I really was. In this
marriage I had lost all sense of myself as an individual—
and so had he."

In a synergistic relationship, both people become greater
through their relationship than either one is capable of
becoming alone. Separately both are reasonably strong,
secure individuals who are content within themselves,
but together their love creates a powerful, nurturing
bond—providing each with more happiness than either
one ever knew existed. While they have both mastered
the skill of making themselves happy on their own, they
realize that sharing their life with the right person can
make them happier. This is a relationship based on a
shared philosophy of life, mutual trust, and reciprocal
giving and taking.

Remember Jennifer, who collapsed on the library floor
of her Malibu mansion and then went into seclusion
when she realized that she had to end her marriage to
Rick? After all the pain that she endured, she emerged
from her loveshock a stronger and more secure individual. When she met Tony she was finally content with
herself and the new life she had created. He too is a

secure individual with lots of interests and a very busy life. Since they have married, neither one of them has lost sight of their individuality. And when they're together, they enhance one another's happiness. Together they create love synergy.

Love synergy is a realistic ideal worth striving for. It is the type of relationship that I hope you will seek. You are certainly capable of attaining it because of the strength, competence, and self-awareness you have gained from your loveshock experience, and which you continue to develop as you travel through loveshock.

But even within the framework of a synergistic love relationship, you must maintain reasonable expectations: even the best relationships involve compromise and trade-offs. What's critical in creating a new relationship, working toward love synergy, is that neither of you compromise what's essential for your personal happiness and emotional well-being.

MAKING LOVE WORK

Often I am asked by loveshock patients who are in resolution and eager to love again, "How can I love again without experiencing loveshock again?" Unfortunately, there are no guarantees. And whenever you choose to love again, you are once again vulnerable to loveshock. This is not pessimism—just reality.

While the topic of making love work is vast and multidimensional, constantly being researched and explored by an increasing number of research scientists and psychologists, one of the best guidelines I have to offer is to approach love realistically. This means removing the *may be* and *could be* from love and dealing with the *what is*. Again, this means realizing that you can't marry the promise.

I'm the first to agree that the different love myths and romantic fantasies are wonderful ideals that can continue to ignite and fan the flames of passion that feed a relationship, but they have very little to do with the actual endurance of relationships. In fact, they may even hurt relationships by creating unrealistic expectations that few partners can live up to.

The reality of love is that it takes personal sacrifices from both partners if it is to be sustained. You must think, act, and react for two people rather than one to create harmony; you must consider your partner's feelings as well as your own. Your wants and needs only count for half of the whole, which is now composed of the two of you. There are endless compromises that must be made. And the moment either of you begins to take love for granted, it begins to end.

Many of you are already aware of the role neglect plays in the demise of a love relationship. Like so many of my loveshock patients, once your relationship was established you may not have continued to nurture it. Your energy was diverted elsewhere—perhaps into raising children or furthering your career. While these are also important, time-consuming parts of life, you cannot deny the demands of a love relationship. And because it usually creates the foundation for the other parts of your life, when it crumbles the rest of your life may begin to fall apart as well.

One of the toughest love lessons most of us have to learn is that lasting relationships don't just fall on us and then flourish on their own. They are created by mutual commitment and they only continue by mutual commitment—and often through very trying times. Without a doubt, the happiest and most enduring relationships are those that receive constant attention and true nurturing. Perhaps this is why the marriage vows, which celebrate and unite the love between two people, also remind us, "for better and for worse; in sickness and in health."

ROMANTIC LOVE AND OTHER TYPES OF LOVE

Resolution brings with it, besides a new life cycle, a serenity that will continue to develop as you grow emotionally stronger every day. Regardless of the direction your new life takes, you now realize that you are strong enough to live and live well on your own. You may wish that you didn't have to, but knowing that you can gives you a greater feeling of personal competence. After all, you have survived loveshock! You can take care of yourself and you are complete within yourself. While you may desire another relationship, it does not require another person to make you happy.

While many of my loveshock patients anticipate reinvesting their emotional energy in another romantic relationship, there are some who choose not to or can't. Elderly people who are widowed are not as likely to actively seek, or have the opportunity for, a romantic relationship. They usually seek companionship through community projects, family members, friends, or pets. Severe health problems also prevent some people from entering into new relationships, at least while they are focusing all of their energy on their recovery.

I've also had loveshock patients discover during the course of their loveshock that their work must and will always come first. Having reached this conclusion, they are convinced that there is no room in their life for a serious love relationship because they will never be able to put the relationship first. When I tell them that this does not have to be true, they are pleasantly shocked!

While it may not sound or seem very romantic, your love relationship does not have to be your first priority to be satisfying and enduring. Your career can come first as long as you and your partner are in agreement and emotionally comfortable with this arrangement.

I've seen many happy love relationships in which the career comes first for both partners or just for one. These relationships work because the balance of career and love was agreed upon at the outset; needs and expectations were clearly expressed as the relationship was established. Mutual agreement and continuing emotional comfort with this decision are crucial.

Since time shared is often minimal, that often-used expression, "It's the quality, not the quantity that counts," applies in this type of relationship. Because your primary energy is focused on your career, you may really have to stretch yourself to be loving and romantic after a long workday. However, I know several career-oriented couples who are convinced that because their time together is so limited, it is all the more exciting when it finally comes.

Whether you choose to invest your love in another person, in your work, in your children, or in a cause—what's important is that you now have the capacity to make this choice freely, unimpaired. Not out of anger, panic, fear, desperation, despair, revenge, or insecurity. To develop this capacity, to choose in strength the direction your life will take, is the essence of overcoming loveshock.

There is an expression in the Italian language that is translated as, "It's never darker than midnight, and after midnight comes a new day." You may know it as, "It's always darkest before the dawn." A part of growth and maturation is developing the courage to ride out the "midnights" of our lives without becoming self-destructive, without giving into bitterness and self-pity, without losing hope in ourselves, but continuing to believe in the promise of our own lives. Remember Albert Schweitzer's observation quoted earlier: "The tragedy of life is what dies inside a man while he lives!" There are certain qualities within us that belong to us alone . . . they are part of our inalienable rights. No one, no event, no lover must ever take them from us.

No matter how terrible you feel at this moment, no matter what stage of loveshock you are in, do not feel sorry for yourself. You must persevere with your courage and ride it out. Don't lose faith in yourself, your ability to overcome loveshock, and the promise of your future. You can be as happy as you make up your mind to be or as miserable as you let yourself become. If you are having problems moving forward and you cannot resolve these difficulties within yourself or with the support of family and friends, recognize you *can* do it, but you cannot do it alone. Seek the professional guidance and support you need.

And now the good news . . . almost all the people whose lives we shared through the pages of this book are happy again today! Indeed, many are much happier now than they could have ever been in the previous relationship. If that relationship had not ended, they would never have found the opportunity for the new happiness they enjoy. Almost all feel they would never want to go back to their former partner. They have grown too much through their loveshock experience. In a very real sense the pain of loveshock has become a positive force in their lives—it made them leave behind an unrewarding relation and move forward into a happier relationship or new commitments to family, careers or self-growth.

Although it took her many years, Queen Victoria had the courage to travel through her loveshock: she chose to return to Buckingham Palace after her self-imposed exile. At last, unimpaired, she was finally able to confront the palace walls that had once housed the love that she and Albert shared. Once again she presided over Parliament, not just ruling effectively, but leading the British Empire to its zenith.

Conclusion

It's been almost a year and a half since Genevieve's hysterical loveshock collapse in the Polo Lounge. She recently sent me a postcard from the Italian countryside that read, "Divorce settlement with Ryan in my favor. Baby Claude is happy and adores Franco. We met three months ago and are made for one another. I think I've finally found true love . . ." According to my calculations, it took her a little over a year to reach resolution, which for her means Franco. This seems pretty fast, but she has always been a fast traveler. Of course she was married to Ryan for only two years, so getting through resignation was probably not too traumatic.

Right now I have three close friends and several acquaintances who are in some stage of loveshock. Pamela was an unwilling rejector when she made her alcoholic husband leave their Vermont farm. But she's opened a gift shop filled with crystals and New Age books and finds that it's the perfect compelling diverter as she moves herself through her loveshock.

My friend Ross has just marked the one-year anniversary of his loveshock, which began when Alicia rejected him after ten years of marriage, and is still struggling through the final stages. He's definitely in rebuilding but suffers from loveshock flashbacks (he still can't eat Chinese food, which Alicia loved), and occasionally he zigzags and picks up the phone to reconnect with her. Actually, I think his biggest problem with loveshock has been integrating the ten-year history they once shared into his new life. I spent a lot of time with him while he was going through resignation and the only things he kept were the photo albums. For such a high-powered advertising executive, his traveling time through love-shock has been slower than I would have expected.

Then there's Jamie, whose girlfriend moved out three months ago. He actually met her when they were in the second grade, and they finally started living together four years ago. He's the first to admit that he's been obsessed with her since the first day they met. Refusing to accept that he has been rejected, Jamie is still locked in his grief and is up to his ears in obsessional thinking and moth-to-flaming. He's turning into an old man before my eyes—and he's only thirty-five! Fortunately, he's started therapy.

And there's Anne—poor Anne—who is about to go into loveshock but doesn't know it yet. I went to college with Anne and all she ever talked about was having a husband, babies, and a home. She ended up marrying Mark, who is ten years older and was one of our professors. He recently called me, confessing that he was having a mid-life crisis and was feeling smothered by everything, including Anne, their four children, and even the dog. Since Anne is one of my best friends, he wanted to know if I had any suggestions—specifically, "How do I break the news to her gently?" All I could answer was, "She'll be devastated." I can't even begin to imagine how long her loveshock will last.

As for me, as Thanksgiving approaches, it's been almost one year since my loveshock hit. Last Thanksgiving my husband and I barely spoke. Our misunderstandings, lack of communication, and personal problems had placed what seemed to be an indestructible wall between us. The only chinks were our two little girls.

We are both in the rebuilding stage of loveshock. *Together*. Given our history, I'm surprised too. But as Dr. Gullo explained in Chapter Three, it is possible to reunite with your partner during rebuilding if there have been drastic changes in behavior and both of you are willing to work at the relationship. Well, we've both made changes and we are working hard to repair the damage to our marital foundation. But the ground rules have been changed. We've become more tolerant of each other's personal needs and we have created an entirely different relationship from what we had. It is a relationship that many people don't understand, but for now it works for us.

Although we are rebuilding together, I still have loveshock flashbacks. Every time I drive by the hospital, I cringe and sometimes take a wrong turn, as I am reminded of the night my marriage finally fell apart. That night my husband, hurt and angry, went out and kicked a wall. He shattered his heel and ankle into too many pieces to count. As I watched him suffer in the emergency room, with my baby in my arms and my young daughter beside me, it made me sick to think that what had started out as love could end like this. Both of us were responsible for this unhappy ending.

While my story is unique. I know now that I'm not alone. Loveshock victims fill the world, as they have throughout history, and each has his or her tragic tale to tell. Without a doubt, going through loveshock is one of life's most traumatic experiences.

But I'm not afraid to love again. Love, no matter how brief, is a miracle to me. There are no guarantees that the cracks have been permanently sealed in my marriage and that my husband and I will spend the rest of our lives together. And even if we do, one of us will have to go through loveshock again because of death. But if or when it happens to me again, I will manage it and move through it better because now I understand it. Now I know that unless it takes a pathological twist, loveshock too has an end. Loveshock is not a mental illness; it is an inevitable process for anyone who suffers a love loss.

As difficult as it has been, my loveshock experience has made me a stronger person. Dr. Gullo's loveshock therapy gave me the courage to manage my pain, as I realized that I had the capacity to cope with the heartache and fear that comes with a profound love loss. While I had to push myself forward and at times had nothing to go on but my self-belief, the result has been an inner awareness of myself and a lot of personal growth that I'm grateful for.

There is no question that Dr. Gullo's loveshock theory and therapy are an invaluable contribution to the mental health field. He has named our pain and seen clearly how to mend a heart that has been broken by a love loss. He has given us loveshock victims hope and shown us that there is a light that shines at the end of that long, dark tunnel. Regardless of your pain, those loveshock days and nights won't last forever, and someday you will be able to love again.

Acknowledgments

Loveshock is not only an evolution of my professional work in the field of loss; it is deeply influenced by my own philosophy of life and loving. In this way it is a product of both my professional and personal life. There are many who have contributed enormously to these aspects of my growth. And so, in a very real way, they have contributed directly to *Loveshock*.

First and foremost, I would like to thank my agent, Al Lowman. This book would never have become a reality without his vision, guidance and deep belief in the value of loveshock therapy.

On a personal note, I owe much to my family: especially my father and my mother, Rose Pernice Gullo, who first taught me the meaning of unconditional love; my sisters, Angela, Marianne and Antoinette, whose sacrifices and commitment nurture me daily and were especially helpful during the many and often laborious years of my professional training; my nephews Christian Hanny and Matthew Touron and my niece Maureen Levine, who enrich my life and give me and my family the opportunity to pass the joys and the responsibilities of loving on to the next generation; my brothers-in-law, who have been so supportive of our family ties and who contribute so much to our family life, especially Joseph Barna and Bob Pahlck and Al Froehlich. Those who have a loving family are blessed.

I owe a special debt of gratitude to the physicians who

helped restore me to the fullness of life after a major illness: Dr. John Conley, one of the giants of American surgery, Dr. Robert De Bellis, Dr. Irwin Dannis, Dr. Irwin Lubowe, Dr. William Shaw and his devoted nurse Irena Ciccone.

Perhaps one of the most enriching aspects of my personal life has been the support and guidance of my dear friends. I owe a great deal to each of you: my life-long friends David and Marilyn Kahn, Richard Berger and Scott Yacker. Also: Ronni Janoff, Mark Lazar, Hal Parkerson, John Contini, Jason Capuano, David Sholtis, Dr. Daniel Cherico, Tony Danaro, Debbie Melendez, and Wilfredo Rivera, Al Galleau, Kurt Barnard, Mike Nelligan, Barry Schneider, Brian Snyder, Lee Ciardiello, Mike and Eric Francis, Howard Sussman, Millie Kenig, David Demattia, and of course my friend Peter Swersey for reminding me of the resilience of the human spirit and what honorable people can accomplish through commitment to growth.

Several other friends have enriched my life, not only through the joys of friendship, but through what they have contributed to my professional growth. As classmates at Columbia, and later as colleagues, they have been a major influence in my life. Dr. Daniel Carr, a brilliant researcher and physician, has been one of my great teachers. It was he who sensitized me and has taught me so much about the biological basis of human behavior. Our discussions continue to enhance my work and our friendship enriches my personal and professional growth. Psychiatrist Dr. Henry Berger helped me to understand much about the role of the rejectee in *Loveshock* and encouraged my *Loveshock* research through his insights and unfailing friendship. Dr. Marc Shatz has provided me with an intellectual form within which to refine my ideas. All of their insights, and most of all, their humanity as caregivers, in the highest tradition, have enriched this book and my capacity to help others.

Thank you to my dear friends: Michael Francis, Burt Primoff, Michael Kalnick, and Fran Brody, who guided and assisted me with their counsel during the formative years of my career. Their advice and friendship has improved the quality of my professional work and my life. And no expression of gratitude would be complete without acknowledging Florence Lazar and Lee Love, who came to my rescue during the first days of my work.

I'd also like to thank several colleagues who assisted me in my early research in the field of loss and generously shared their insights, including: Dr. Ivan Goldberg, Dr. Robert De Bellis, and the late Dr. Bernard Schoenberg. Also, the late Dr. Boyd McCandless.

I am grateful for the honors bestowed on me and my work by his Royal Imperial Highness, Prince Robert Khimchiavelli von Badische, Sir John Tewder-Reese, Ambassador Sir Victor Tewder-Reese, and the Honorable Ruggero Orlando.

A special thanks to my colleagues, with whom I work on a daily basis: Rosemarie Passaro, my wonderful administrative assistant and bookkeeper; my long-time colleague, Dr. Jerome Feldman; Dr. Robert Lipman and Dr. John Gross, for all that they contribute both to my life and to my work; Dr. Richard Corriere and Dr. Ruth Westheimer, whose counsel has enriched my work and enhanced my ability to use my talents to help others.

Also, my appreciation for two individuals who built the house that I designed in Southhampton, which has been my refuge and my haven wherein I found the serenity to formulate my ideas on *Loveshock:* Alex Dzieman, master builder, and Tim Suttmeier, whose dedication and resourcefulness made my house a reality.

A special thanks to my personal assistants, Lonnie Quinn and Norbert Bogner, who keep me organized and help my life run smoothly.

And finally, thank you to Jim, Eleanor, and Marisa Walker, for understanding and enduring all the long hours my coauthor, Connie Church, spent away from home.

—STEPHEN GULLO

In writing *Loveshock,* many professionals, loved ones, and close friends played an important part in its creation. I would like to thank all of you for opening up your hearts and sharing your loveshock experiences with me.

I would also like to thank my two dear friends, Marisa Berenson and Zoe Artemis, for sharing their homes with me and providing me with the solitude I needed. Also, thank you both for your constant love and support— especially during those dark days when my creative muse vanished.

A special thanks to Gerald Jackson, for his unconditional friendship which adds so much to my life and has guided me out of more than one pitfall.

And, finally, a special thanks to my family, for loving me—even when you didn't approve—and for just being there.

—CONNIE CHURCH

We would both like to deeply thank all those who played a vital role in the creation of this book:

Our wonderful editor, Bob Bender, for his guidance and patience. With the help of his editorial expertise, this book stayed on course and made its deadline—just in the nick of time.

Also to Brian Moore, Betsy Lerner, and Behrman Communications for your assistance during all stages of this book.

Murry Rogow, for his help and contribution in the initial stages of creating this book.

And, Patricia Soliman and Joni Evans, who helped bring *Loveshock* and Simon and Schuster together. And, to our Canadian publisher, Jan Whitford, at Collins, Canada.